D0568409

THE VEGETABLE GARDENER'S BOOK OF **BUILDING** PROJECTS

FROM THE EDITORS OF STOREY PUBLISHING

THE VEGETABLE GARDENER'S BOOK OF BUILDING PROJECTS

**Raised Beds • Cold Frames • Compost Bins
Planters • Plant Supports • Trellises
Harvesting and Storage Aids**

Projects designed and built by Kevin Ayer
Text edited by Cindy A. Littlefield
Photography by John Gruen

Storey Publishing

*The mission of Storey Publishing is to serve our customers by
publishing practical information that encourages
personal independence in harmony with the environment.*

Edited by Gwen Steege
Art direction and book design by Mary Winkelman Velgos

Photography by © John Gruen
Photo styling by Lisa Newman
Illustrations © Michael Gellatly

Indexed by Nancy D. Wood

Storey Publishing
210 MASS MoCA Way
North Adams, MA 01247
www.storey.com

Printed in the United States by Versa Press
10 9 8 7 6 5 4 3 2

Library of Congress Cataloging-in-Publication Data

The vegetable gardener's book of building projects / by the Editors of Storey Publishing.
   p. cm.
 Includes index.
 ISBN 978-1-60342-526-1 (pbk. : alk. paper)
 1. Gardening—Equipment and supplies. 2. Garden ornaments and furniture.
 3. Vegetable gardening. I. Storey Communications.
SB454.8.V44 2010
635—dc22
                              2010000844

To vegetable gardeners everywhere:
May your peas and beans scramble high,
your tomatoes hang heavy on their vines,
your berries be plump and sweet,
and all of your harvests be tasty and bountiful!

Many thanks to the gardeners who generously "hosted" the projects in this book,
giving each of them a trial run in a real garden:
Judith Bowerman and Larry Slezak, Judy and John Dolven,
Robert Horton, Diane Krok, and Gloria Pacosa; also
to Forest Product Associates in
Greenfield, Massachusetts, who
supplied props for photo shoots.

CONTENTS

CREATING A WELL-BUILT GARDEN

Like most chosen pastimes, gardening is inherently rewarding. It inspires creativity from the moment you start planning the plot; it provides enjoyable outdoor exercise while you tend seedlings and vines; and it culminates in a deep sense of satisfaction when you harvest and feast on juicy tomatoes, crunchy beans and peas, and all the other fresh vegetables your plantings bear.

Still, as with any labor of love, having the proper tools and equipment goes a long way toward keeping the joys of gardening in the forefront. Be it a cold frame for getting a jump on the season, a rack for storing rakes and shovels, or a sturdy, lightweight box for gathering newly picked produce, the right prop can save you time, effort, and frustration. In this book you'll find plans for 39 woodworking projects that fit the bill. Many are meant to be used specifically in or for the garden. Others (birdhouses and feeders, lawn chairs, and a bench-style swing) are designed to complement it by transforming your yard into a haven for wildlife and a place to sit back and survey your handiwork at the end of the day.

While some of the projects can be made easily by beginning woodworkers in a couple of hours, some will provide satisfying challenges for more experienced craftspeople. To ensure success, all the plans feature a shopping list of materials (including the types and lengths of wood you'll need to request at the lumberyard) and step-by-step illustrated instructions for cutting the boards and assembling the pieces. In addition, throughout the book you'll find helpful building tips pertaining to specific projects.

Before getting started, take a few minutes to read the following general woodworking advice. And if a question crops up during the building process, don't be afraid to run it by a local craftsperson or trade-school teacher you may know. Many people versed in woodworking are happy to share their knowledge. You can probably find a lot of answers and tips online as well. By the time you've completed a project or two, you just may discover that you have a brand-new hobby.

Tools and Materials

Using the right tools for each woodworking project lets you work efficiently and ensures the best results. The same holds true for materials. Good-quality exterior hardware, for example, will hold up for a long time, making it well worth the investment. Here are some points to consider.

POWER TOOLS VERSUS HAND TOOLS

While you can make most cuts with hand tools in a pinch, power tools certainly make the job easier and more efficient. For example, using a power miter saw allows you to set the desired angle and cut a bunch of balusters in much less time, and more accurately, than if you were to mark the angle on each board individually.

You can build most of the projects in this book using a circular saw (preferably one with a rip guard), but a table saw is ideal. And for curved cuts a jigsaw makes for an easier job than a coping saw would. A jigsaw can also be used in lieu of a circular saw, which may be intimidating to use for beginners. One tool you won't want to be without is a power drill, corded or cordless (which is convenient but not as powerful as a plug-in style).

BLADES

When cutting wood, remember that sharp saw blades are easier to use and cut straighter than dull ones. Using a dull blade (be it on a handsaw or a power saw) can actually be dangerous because you have to apply more force than is ordinarily necessary to push it through the wood. The same applies to chisels and utility knives.

SQUARES

When building, a square is indispensable. The classic carpenter's square is a large L-shaped piece of aluminum or steel and is particularly handy for large-scale projects. A combination square is smaller but more versatile, with a sliding ruler that can be used to mark 45° and 90° angles. A speed square can also come in handy for some projects. It is triangular in shape and pivots so you can mark any angle. Using a carpenter's square to mark your cuts will ensure they are straight.

FASTENERS AND HARDWARE

In most cases screws are a better choice than nails for a tighter hold — an asset for outdoor projects that are subject to humidity and temperature changes, which make the wood expand and contract, eventually popping the nails. The threads of the screws keep them tight. Screws are also more forgiving; if something needs adjusting, you can more easily unscrew a board than remove the nails. In general, use larger screws for structural and framing components and smaller, more decorative screws for finish pieces and surfaces.

A couple of the projects in this book call for a *continuous hinge*, also known as a *piano hinge* because it was developed to use on keyboard lids. This style of hinge doesn't need to be recessed and, being relatively thin, is well suited for attaching to a ¾" board. Continuous hinges are sold in most hardware stores and come in several standard sizes. You can use a hacksaw to cut one to the specific length required for a given project.

While you should be able to find the fasteners and hardware you need locally, there are some helpful online sources, too. McFeely's (www.mcfeelys.com) specializes in hard-to-find tools and hardware. Rockler Woodworking and Hardware (www.rockler.com) and Woodworker's Supply (http://woodworker.com) are a couple of other good sources.

Safety First

When working with wood, keep a first-aid kit handy and dress comfortably but not in loose clothing — you don't want a sleeve or shirttail to inadvertently get caught in a power tool. Invest in a good pair of work gloves (the ones coated with rubber for a better grip). Not only do these help you avoid getting splinters, but they are also indispensable when handling wire mesh. Eye protection is a must. Always wear safety goggles and a dust mask when cutting or sanding wood. Wear earplugs, too, when using power tools. Even repetitive hammering can take a toll on your hearing. Above all, respect the power of the tools you're using, take your time, and stay focused on what you're doing, rather than thinking about the next step or a phone call you want to make.

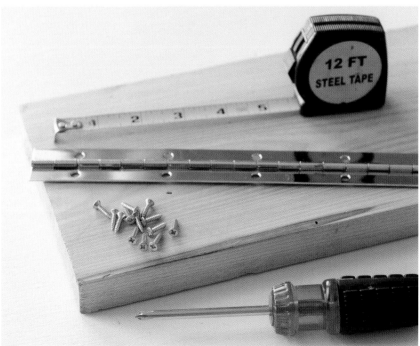

Lumber and Finishes

Once you start working with wood, you will be amazed at how many varieties are available. When selecting one, be sure to consider more than cost. Durability, how easy it is to work with, and aesthetics are important, too. Your choice will also depend on how, or if, you plan on finishing the wood.

CHOOSING THE RIGHT WOOD

A primary consideration for any woodworking project is choosing a type of wood that's well suited to it. Most of the projects on the following pages were built with cedar, which is a good choice for exterior woodworking, since it is lightweight yet very durable. Besides its being naturally resistant to decay, the bugs don't seem to like it. And if you choose to forgo a finish and let it weather, it will turn a silvery gray. Cedar is also a smooth wood, which makes it nice for seating. To save money, instead of buying clear cedar, you can purchase a slightly lesser grade and cut around the knots.

Other native woods that make good choices for outdoor projects include white oak, bald cypress, honey locust, and redwood, although you may not be able to find them in every region. When choosing wood, if in doubt, it's always a good idea to consult with your local lumberyard representative.

WOOD PRESERVATIVES

The easiest and most environmentally friendly option is to use no finish and allow the wood to naturally weather. This option works best with woods such as cedar, redwood, and cypress, which tend to be more resistant to rot. Ipê, an exotic hardwood from South America that is increasingly being used for decking and wooden bridges, is exceptionally hard and fares quite well unpreserved. Still, the elements will eventually take a toll on any untreated wood. Sunlight alone causes wood to chemically degrade, and the cycle of absorbing moisture and drying out invariably produces cracks. Applying the right finish can help prolong the life and aesthetic appeal of outdoor woodworking projects.

Assuming you wish to keep the grain of the wood visible, you'll want a clear preservative. Marine-grade varnishes yield the best results, effectively preventing the wood from cracking and preserving the brightness of the wood. Although widely used, polyurethanes and oils tend to be considerably less effective.

One Box, Four Different Colors, Four Different Looks

Instead of using a clear preservative to protect your window box, you may prefer to paint it. This opens dozens of design possibilities, and if you can't make up your mind, you can easily change the color the next year — or the next season — for an entirely different look. You might want to paint the box the same color as your house or choose a complementary color. It's just as important and as much fun to choose a color scheme that coordinates with the plants you are growing. For best results, be sure to use outdoor paint.

General Building Tips

As with any trade, there are building techniques and tricks that make the job go more smoothly. Here are a few general pointers that will help ensure your woodworking experience is successful and pleasurable.

● **Consider custom cutting.** Often, lumberyards will cut the wood you purchase to the lengths you want or, at a minimum, to lengths that are easier to transport home. Be aware that there may be a charge for this service.

● **Allow for saw waste.** When laying out cutting lines on lumber, keep in mind that the saw will pulverize a blade's width of wood with each cut. This means, for example, you won't be able to cut four 2' lengths out of an 8' length; you'll need to buy a little extra or size the project to accommodate standard lengths of lumber. Also, always cut on the "waste" side of the cutting line — don't let the saw blade eat up any of the wood on the length you've just measured.

● **Allow for finished lumber size.** Keep in mind, too, that common finished lumber is named by the size of the rough lumber, but by the time it is milled and planed to the finish boards you actually buy, it can be ¼" to ¾" smaller. A 2"x4", for example, actually measures 1½"x3½".

● **Predrill nail and screw holes.** Whenever practical, it's a good idea to predrill holes for screws and nails to minimize the chance that the wood will split and to make it easier to start them. To determine where to set nails and screws, generally you measure in half the distance of the wood thickness. For example, when fastening together two boards that are 1" thick, place the screws ½" inch in from the edge.

● **Mark up layouts.** When laying out marks where one or more boards will attach to a series of parallel boards (such as where the pickets attach to the rails of a gate), rather than measuring and marking each of the parallel boards individually, mark one board. Then place the other boards up against the first, flushing up the ends, and use the markings as a guide for penciling markings onto the other boards. This minimizes the likelihood of measuring incorrectly, and it can save a lot of time.

● **Use a utility knife.** Score a cutting line before you saw it. This will help avoid splintering and make for a more precise cut.

● **Round off edges.** The edges of a piece of lumber, especially a length that is freshly cut, are often sharper than you may imagine. You can remedy this by rounding the edges. This can be done simply with a sanding block or a wood file. Another option is to bevel them with a wood plane or a chisel. And to round the edges on larger projects, such as outdoor furniture, a router fitted with a flush round-over bit comes in handy. In some cases, clipping the corners of boards (cutting them at a 45° angle), such as on the Berry Box (page 86), is an effective method and can also lend the project a decorative flair.

● **Countersink screws and bolts.** Countersinking (fastening the screws or bolts so that the heads are flush with or just below the surface of the wood) allows you to keep the surface of your woodworking project smooth. To do this, you drill a shallow hole in the wood surface to suit the head (flat or tapered) where the screw goes. This is particularly important in locations where you don't want the heads to protrude and be a hazard. Some screws, such as pan-head screws, have flat-bottomed heads and don't need to be countersunk. The head of this style of screw presses down evenly on the wood, making a particularly strong joint.

1 | BUILDING PROJECTS FOR
PLANTING
AND
GROWING

Window Sash Cold Frame

Using a cold frame can extend your growing season four to six weeks on each end. Here is a good model that is straightforward to build, small enough to reach into easily yet large enough to help in your gardening, and a great use for any spare window sashes you may have on hand.

MATERIALS

Lumber

2"×4" cedar (10' length)

1"×6" cedar (12' length and 16' length)

1"×8" cedar (6' length)

1"×10" cedar (8' length)

Two tomato stakes (27" lengths)

Two 30"×29" window sashes

Supplies

Two pairs of 3½"×2½" exterior hinges and screws to go with them

2" exterior wood screws (70 or so)

Two 1⅝" exterior wood screws

Tools

Tape measure

Pencil

Carpenter's square

Wood saw

Power drill

⁵⁄₃₂" twist drill bit

Driver bit to match screws

Temperature

With a cold frame, the danger of heat and dehydration is far greater than the danger of cold, even during the early spring and late fall when you will be using your cold frame the most. Remember that even on the coldest winter day, the bright sun can quickly push the temperature in the cold frame up to above 75°-80°F (24°-27°C), which should be the maximum. Provide a system of props so that, if there is a chance of overheating, the sash can be raised. Unless prevailing winds blow directly into the cold frame, there is little danger of damaging plants through chilling them.

▲ WINDOW SASH COLD FRAME. Old window sashes are ready-made tops for this style of cold frame. If you don't have any spare sashes, you can frequently find overstock for sale at your local lumber store.

Cutting the lumber. From the 2"×4", cut three 19½" lengths Ⓐ and three 12½" lengths Ⓑ for the upright posts.

From the 1"×6", cut three 59½" lengths for the lower front and back boards Ⓒ and five 25½" lengths for the side and center boards Ⓓ.

From the 1"×8", cut one 59½" length for the upper front Ⓔ.

From the 1"×10", cut boards for the upper back Ⓕ and angled upper sides Ⓖ as specified in the cutting diagram at right.

BUILDER'S TIP

The dimensions for this style of cold frame revolve around the window sashes you use. If yours are a different size than the 30"×29" ones specified here, you'll have to modify the frame accordingly. Either way, attaching the sashes with hinges that have loose pins will allow you to remove the windows easily if needed.

Cutting diagram

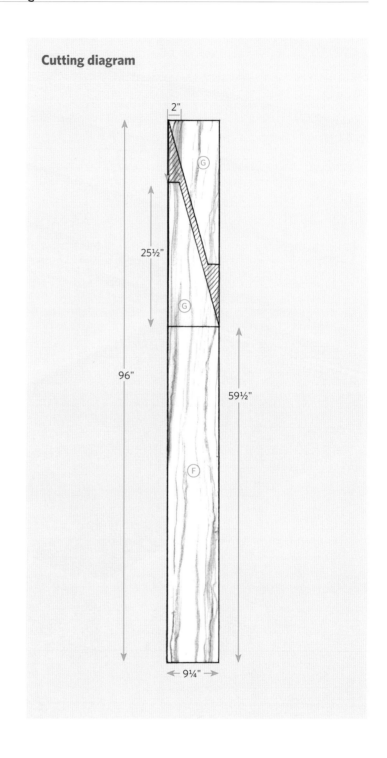

Constructing the cold frame. To start, build the side panels using the taller upright posts Ⓐ for the back corners and the shorter upright posts Ⓑ for the front corners. The angled upper sides Ⓖ will create a sloped top that both permits rainfall to run off the cold frame and allows for maximum sunlight to reach the plants inside. Screw the front boards Ⓒ & Ⓔ and back boards Ⓒ & Ⓕ to the ends of the side boards Ⓓ & Ⓖ to create a box. Then attach the center posts Ⓐ & Ⓑ to the inner box and screw the ends of the center board Ⓓ to them.

Position the window sashes on the frame so that the tops are flush with the back wall (they will overhang the sides and front of the frame a bit), and mount the hinges. To provide ventilation, use the 1⅝" screws to attach the bottoms of the tomato stakes to the inner front corners of the frame, as shown. The screws should be loose enough to allow the sticks to pivot forward when you want to prop the frame open.

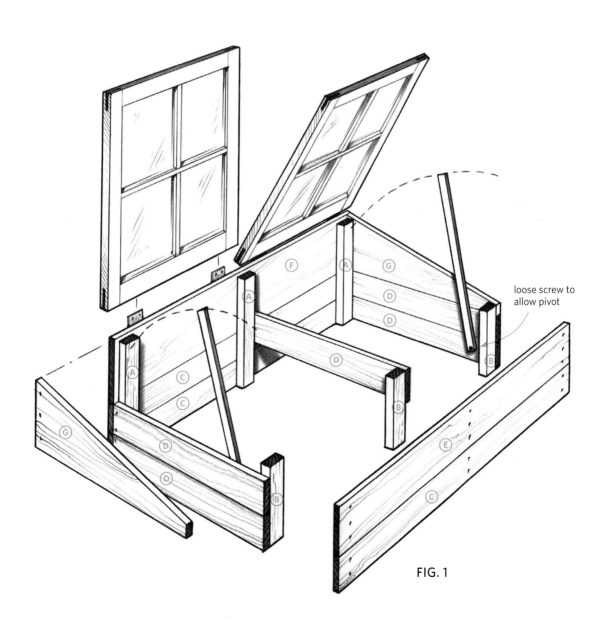

loose screw to allow pivot

FIG. 1

Shallow Raised Bed

MATERIALS

Lumber
2"×8" cedar (two 12' lengths)

Supplies
Twenty-four 3" galvanized
    wood screws

Tools
Tape measure
Pencil
Carpenter's square
Wood saw
Power drill
5⁄32" twist drill bit
Driver bit to match screws

When conventional gardening is not an option — if you don't have the space, perhaps, or the right kind of soil — raised beds are often a viable, if not advantageous, alternative. Beds with conservative widths (3'–5') allow you to reach into the middle to plant or weed without ever stepping on, and thus compacting, the soil. And the bench seats at the ends allow you to sit comfortably, as opposed to bending over while tending the bed.

Preparing the Bed for Planting

While you can simply fill a raised bed with soil once it is built, doing some prior ground preparation will produce much better results. Once you've chosen a location (a spot that will provide full sun is ideal), remove any turf. Next, dig down, turning over a couple feet of subsoil. Finally, fill the bed with a good mixture of soil, compost, and manure, and level the surface.

▲ SHALLOW RAISED BED. The built-in benches on this handy planter provide a convenient and comfortable perch for tending your plants.

Cutting the lumber. Cut the cedar into two 72" lengths for the long sides Ⓐ, two 33" lengths for the short sides Ⓑ, and two 36" lengths for benches Ⓒ.

Constructing the bed. Create a rectangular frame by fastening the long sides Ⓐ to the short sides Ⓑ, as shown. Then set the bench seats Ⓒ atop the frame, flushing up the edges, and fasten them in place.

Setting up the bed. Locate the bed where it will catch full sun if possible. Mark off the size of the bed with stakes and string. Then use a shovel to dig down and remove all sod, grass, and weeds.

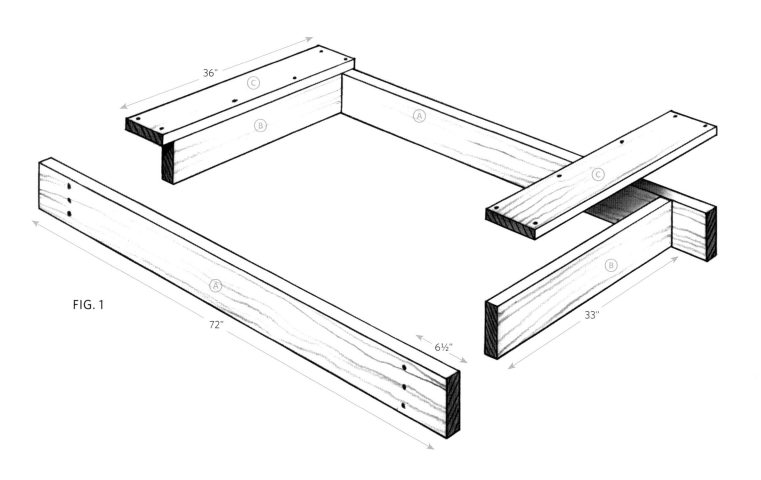

FIG. 1

BUILDER'S TIP

Adding bench boards to the ends of the raised bed not only provides a comfortable seat for weeding but also serves to strengthen the corners.

Deep Raised Bed

What's nice about a deep raised bed is that there is no need to remove the sod underneath it. You can simply fill it with soil and start planting.

▼ DEEP RAISED BED. A deep bed, such as this one, holds enough soil to keep plantings moist for longer stretches of time than a shallow bed would.

MATERIALS

Lumber
4"×6" Douglas fir
   (ten 8' lengths)

Supplies
Fifty-six 6" timber-lock
   screws

Tools
Tape measure
Pencil
Carpenter's square
Wood saw
Heavy power drill
½" spade drill bit
⅛" extra-long twist drill
   bit
Driver bit that comes with
   the screws

Cutting the lumber. Cut the 4"×6" into ten 65¾" lengths for the long sides Ⓐ and ten 29¾" lengths for the short sides Ⓑ.

Constructing the bed. Assemble the first layer on the ground by using two longer lengths Ⓐ and two shorter lengths Ⓑ to form a rectangle, as shown in fig. 1. Lay a second layer atop the first, alternating the timbers in the corners so that the joints are staggered (fig. 2). To prevent the wood from splitting, predrill holes, ½" deep and ½" wide, for the screws in the top layer, following the pattern provided in fig. 2. Then fasten down the wood, countersinking the screws so they are flush with the surface. Continue in this way, adding three more layers to the planter for a total of five layers.

BUILDER'S TIPS

Turn the boards so the best face is showing. When fastening each layer, flush up the edges and tack the four corners together before sinking the other screws.

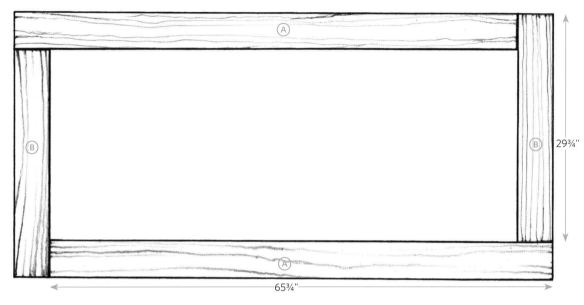

FIG. 1

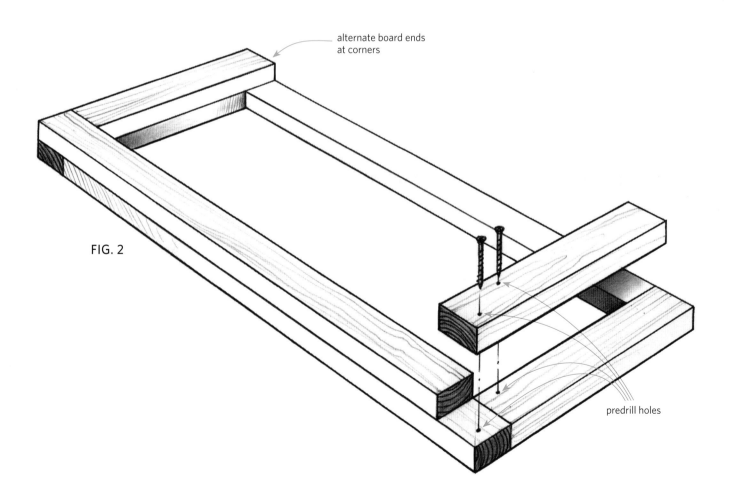

alternate board ends at corners

predrill holes

FIG. 2

Classic Compost Bin

MATERIALS

Lumber

Two dozen 2"×2"×36" cedar balusters

Supplies

Four pieces of 36"×38½" hardware cloth (with ½" squares)

Sixty 2½" pan-head exterior screws

Two pounds ¾" galvanized poultry staples

Eight 2½"-long hook-and-eye latches

Tools

Tape measure

Pencil

Carpenter's square

Combination square

Wood saw

Power drill

⁵⁄₃₂" and ⅛" twist drill bits

Driver bit to match screws

Staple gun

Work gloves

Awl

Pliers

Two clamps and wood blocks

Tin snips

Hammer

This type of compost bin has been a popular choice for many years. It is easy to assemble and use — particularly when the compost is ready to turn. You simply take the sides apart, reassemble them beside the compost pile, and fork the pile back into the bin.

Turning the Pile

As is the case with many things, when it comes to compost bins, the simplest option is often the best. A prime selling point of this style of bin is that the mesh sides allow ample air circulation around the pile, which helps facilitate the aerobic bacterial action of breaking down the organic matter. Once a thermometer inserted into the pile reaches 110°-120°F (43°-49°C), turning the compost every three days or so helps hasten the decomposition process. When the pile reaches 140°-160°F (60°-71°C) and ceases heating up after being turned, the compost is fairly well sterilized and ready to use.

▲ CLASSIC COMPOST BIN. Made with hardware cloth, this bin is lightweight yet durable and provides maximum air circulation.

Cutting the lumber. Cut the balusters into sixteen 36" lengths for framing the bin Ⓐ & Ⓑ. Cut sixteen corner braces Ⓒ with 45° angled ends; the braces should measure 18" from tip to tip.

Constructing the bin. Assemble each of the four panels, as shown in fig. 1, first attaching the upright balusters Ⓑ to the ends of the top and bottom balusters Ⓐ. It's easier if you predrill the screw holes. Then fasten the four corner braces Ⓒ in place. Working on a flat surface, attach a piece of hardware cloth to each panel, stapling every 3½" or so along the perimeter and the braces. Use pliers to pull the cloth taut as you work.

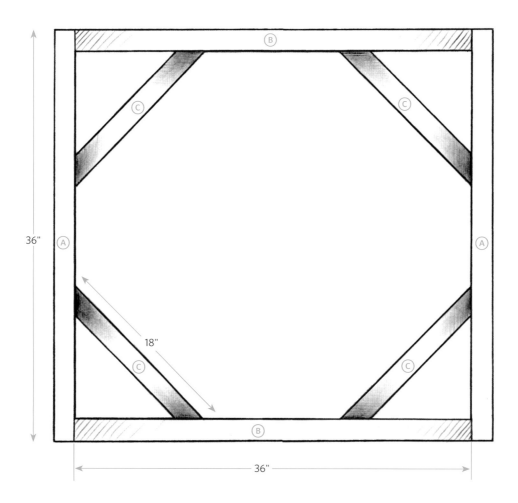

FIG. 1

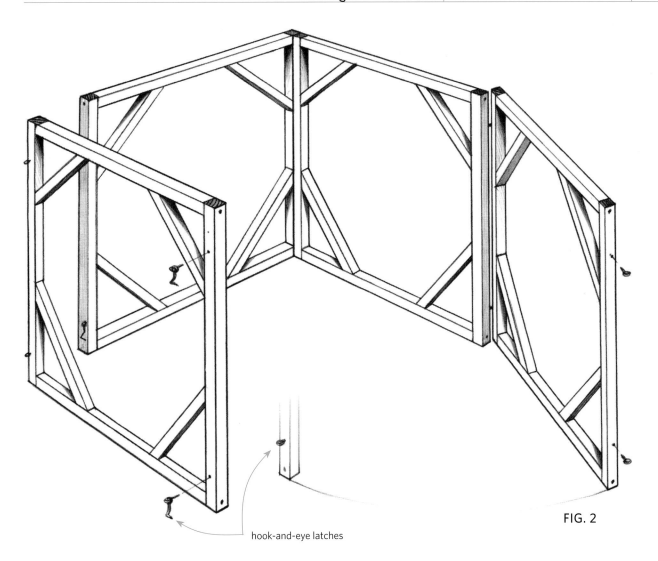

hook-and-eye latches

FIG. 2

Attach the panels to one another with hook-and-eye latches positioned 6" from the tops and the bottoms as in fig. 2. You can make a handy template for predrilling holes for the latches by marking spots 2¼" apart on the back of a business card and then holding the card against the wood and using an awl to poke through the card into the wood. Drill the holes with a ⅛" bit, angling them slightly toward the center of the wood (see fig. 3).

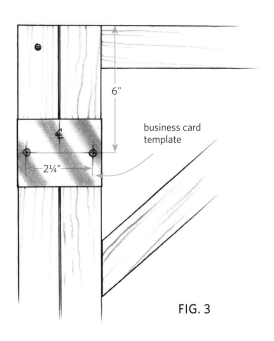

6"

business card
template

2¼"

FIG. 3

New Zealand Compost Box

MATERIALS

Lumber

1"×6" cedar (thirteen 8' lengths)

Ten 2"×2"×3' cedar balusters

Supplies

One hundred and twelve 1⅝" galvanized wood screws

Four 1¼" galvanized wood screws

Tools

Tape measure

Pencil

Carpenter's square

Wood saw

Power drill

$\frac{5}{32}$" twist drill bit

Driver bit to match screws

Hammer

With this style bin, the composting material is less visible and three of the slatted walls are stationary (fastened to stakes in the ground). The front panel, however, is composed of boards that slide in and out to make the work of filling and emptying the box, as well as turning the material, easy.

Compost Materials

One of the great things about composting is the broad range of materials you can use to build the pile. Some of the more common choices include lawn clippings, spoiled hay, garden refuse, kitchen garbage, wood ashes, and leaves. Almost anything organic will do, and the greater the variety, the better the pile. However, some items, such as meat, eggs, dairy products, and grease, can attract rodents and are best avoided. It's also advisable to forgo any herbicide-treated plants.

▲ NEW ZEALAND COMPOST BOX. The slatted sides of this box provide adequate air circulation while reducing the visibility of the composting material inside it.

Cutting and drilling the lumber. From the 1"×6", cut a 59¼" length Ⓐ and two 5" blocks Ⓑ for the support bar, as well as twenty-four 47¾" lengths for the bin slats. Then predrill screw holes in six slats Ⓒ for the back of the bin and twelve slats Ⓓ for the sides, as shown in the cutting diagram. The remaining six slats Ⓕ will be for the front of the bin. Use four of the cedar balusters to create stakes Ⓖ by tapering the ends to points.

Constructing the box. Begin by building the three fixed panels. Start with the back, laying two inside corner balusters Ⓔ on a flat surface and attaching the six back slats Ⓒ to them. Screw the first slat flush to the top ends and side edges of the corners and the second slat ½" up from the bottom. Then fill in the space between them with the remaining four slats, spacing them about ½" apart. (See fig. 1.)

Next, make up the two side panels, but this time screw the front ends of the side slats Ⓓ to one inside corner baluster Ⓔ (which will be positioned at the front of the bin) and leave the back ends of the slats unscrewed. (You will attach them to the back panel once you locate the bin.)

Drive two stakes Ⓖ into the ground about 37" apart where you want the back of the bin to stand. Lean the back panel against the stakes (the stakes should be on the outside of the bin), and screw the panel to the stakes. Then lean the side panels in place, and fasten the loose ends to the inside corner posts Ⓔ of the back panels. (See fig. 1.)

Create a channel in the front corner of each side panel for installing the removable slats that will make up the bin's front panel. To do this, attach another corner post Ⓔ parallel to the existing one, spacing the two just far enough apart for a slat Ⓕ to slide between them. (See fig. 1.)

Cutting diagram

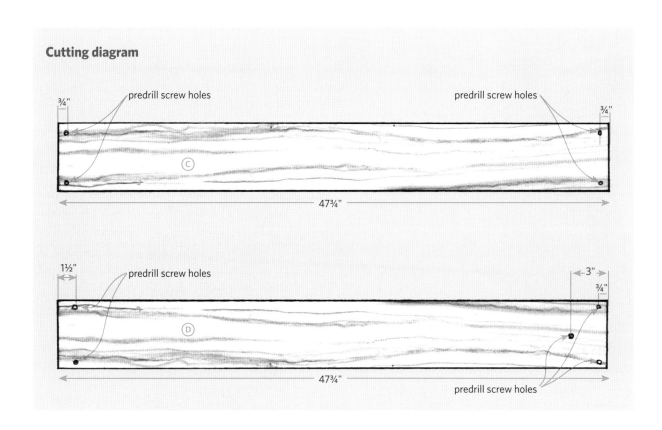

¾"

predrill screw holes

predrill screw holes

¾"

Ⓒ

47¾"

1½"

predrill screw holes

3"

¾"

Ⓓ

47¾"

predrill screw holes

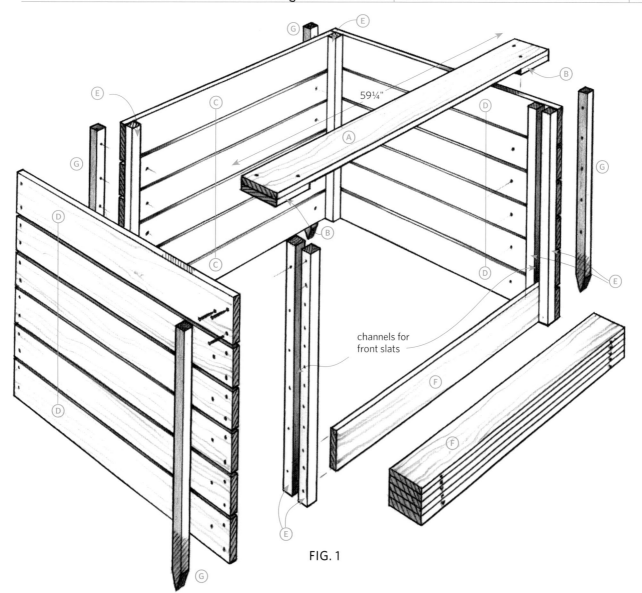

59¼"

channels for
front slats

FIG. 1

Next, partially sink 1⅝" screws into either bottom edge of the six front slats Ⓕ so that the heads are ½" above the wood (fig. 2). The screws will keep the boards properly spaced. Slide the slats down through the channels (with the screwed edges down). Finally, use the 1¼" screws to fasten a support block Ⓑ to each end of the support bar Ⓐ and set the bar across the top of the bin to keep the sides from spreading. Drive a stake Ⓖ into the ground on each side of the bin, and fasten the bin to it from the inside.

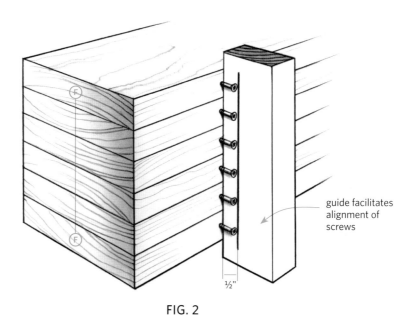

guide facilitates
alignment of
screws

½"

FIG. 2

Small Sifter

A joy of gardening is to work with screened compost when starting tiny plants or transplanting or repotting houseplants. This small sifter is ideal for one person to handle and should be sufficient for a modest garden. Just shake it back and forth, and the finer compost will fall to the ground, ready to use, while the rejected material remains in the sifter and can be returned to the compost pile.

▼ SMALL SIFTER. A box-size sifter is lightweight enough for one person to handle and more than adequate to process compost for a smaller garden.

MATERIALS

Lumber

⁵⁄₄"×6" knotty cedar decking
    (6' length)

Supplies

Eight 2½" exterior decking
    screws
12"×18" piece of hardware
    cloth (with ½" squares)
Handful of ½" galvanized
    staples

Tools

Tape measure
Pencil
Carpenter's square
Power drill
³⁄₁₆" twist drill bit
Driver bit to match screws
Staple gun
Tin snips
Hammer
Work gloves

Cutting the lumber. Cut the decking into two 18" lengths for the long sides Ⓐ and two 10" lengths for the short sides Ⓑ.

Constructing the sifter. Attach the long sides Ⓐ to the ends of the short sides Ⓑ, first predrilling the screw holes. Then stretch the hardware cloth across the frame, and staple it along the edges.

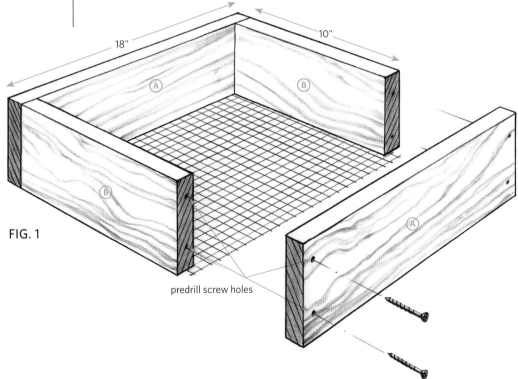

18"   10"

FIG. 1

predrill screw holes

BUILDER'S TIP

Nailing thin strips of wood over the edges of the hardware cloth will further strengthen the sifter and prevent the mesh ends from catching on your work gloves.

Large Sifter

This style of sifter is a good choice if you plan on processing a fair amount of material. To use it, you can either station one person on each end and rock it back and forth or use the stand to prop the sifter at an angle and shovel compost onto it.

▼ LARGE SIFTER. The right equipment makes all the difference when sifting compost. This style is designed to process several large shovelfuls at a time.

Cutting diagram

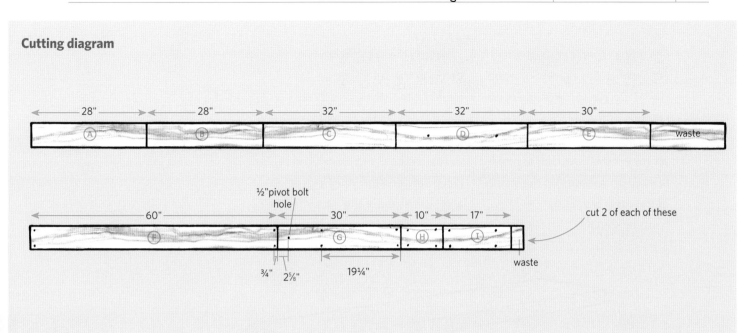

MATERIALS

Lumber

2"×6" cedar (14' length)

⅝"×6" cedar (two 10' lengths)

Supplies

Two 4"×½" bolts with two nuts
and four washers to match

Twenty-two 2½" deck screws

2½'×5' piece of hardware
cloth (with ½" squares)

One box of ¾" galvanized
staples

Sixteen 1½" wood screws for
the pivot block and inner
legs

Tools

Tape measure

Pencil

Carpenter's square

Wood saw

Power drill

½" and ⁵⁄₃₂" twist drill bits

Driver bit to match screws

Adjustable wrench

Staple gun

Tin snips

Hammer

Work gloves

Cutting the lumber. From the 14'
2"×6", cut one 28" length for the
sifter front Ⓐ, one 28" length for
the sifter back Ⓑ, one 32" length
for the stand top Ⓒ, one 32"
length for the stand bottom Ⓓ,
and one 30" length for the stand
brace Ⓔ. From the two 10' lengths
of ⅝"×6", cut two 60" lengths
for the sifter sides Ⓕ, two 30"
lengths for the stand outer legs
Ⓖ, two 10" lengths for the pivot
blocks Ⓗ, and two 17" lengths for
the stand inner legs Ⓘ.

Constructing the sifter. Attach
the sifter sides Ⓕ to the sifter
front Ⓐ and back Ⓑ to construct
the sifter box, making sure the
bottom edges of the wood are
flush. Stretch the hardware cloth
across the frame, and staple it
along the edges.

Working with the box upside
down, attach a pivot block Ⓗ
to the center of one of the sifter
sides Ⓕ. Then stand an outer leg
Ⓖ upright against the block, and
temporarily tack it in place so you

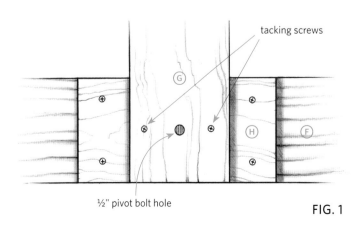

FIG. 1

can drill a ½" hole through the center of all three layers of wood (fig. 1). Do the same on the opposite side of the box.

Remove the tacking screws, and insert the pivot bolt assemblies (with washers on the inside of the sifter box, under the nuts), hand-tightening them for now.

Attach the stand bottom Ⓓ between the outer legs Ⓖ. To reinforce the stand, attach the stand top Ⓒ to the outer legs Ⓖ (fig 2).

Fasten the stand brace Ⓔ in place between the inner leg Ⓘ and against the stand bottom Ⓓ.

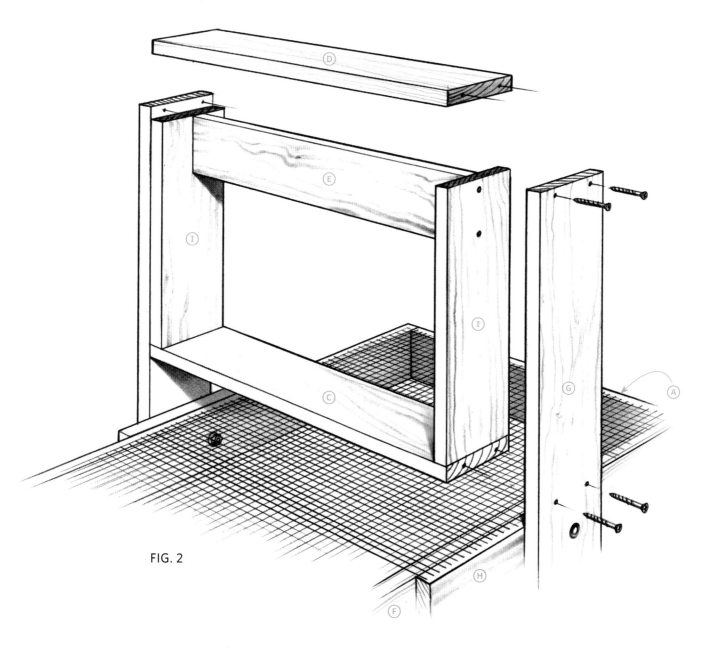

FIG. 2

Circle Plant Support

Most plants benefit one way or another by being supported. Keeping tomatoes, squashes, and other fleshy vegetables off the ground reduces the possibility of mold and rot caused by dampness or fungus in the earth. And with the stalks and leaves off the ground, you can more easily apply mulch.

▼ CIRCLE PLANT SUPPORT. This simple support trains plants to grow upright, conserving considerable space and allowing you to grow more on less land.

MATERIALS

Lumber
Three tomato stakes
(4' long)

Supplies
Heavy-gauge wire
Light-gauge wire

Tools
Tape measure
Pencil
Wire cutter
Wood saw
Pliers
Power drill
½" twist drill bit
Hammer

Constructing the support. Drill holes in the stakes (fig. 1). Thread heavy-gauge wire through the upper set of holes. While keeping the stakes side by side, shape the wire into a 20"-wide circle, overlapping the ends by a couple of inches. Tightly bind the overlapped ends with light-gauge wire. Likewise, create two more circles by threading wire through the middle and lower sets of holes. Then spread the stakes equally apart along the wires.

Using your plant support. When you're ready to install your plant support in its garden location, simply use a hammer to drive the stakes into the ground. To store the supports, you can slide all the stakes together and the wire shapes will drop down and lie flat.

Variation
TRIANGLE PLANT SUPPORT

Follow the instructions for constructing a circle plant support, but shape the heavy-gauge wire into triangles with 17" sides (fig. 2). To do this, it's helpful to use a 17"-long piece of scrap wood with 30° angled cuts on the ends to bend the wire against.

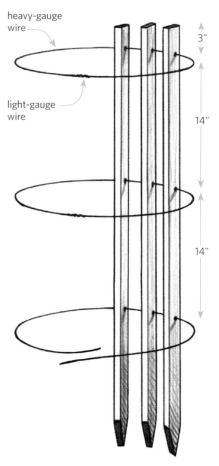

heavy-gauge wire

light-gauge wire

3"

14"

14"

FIG. 1

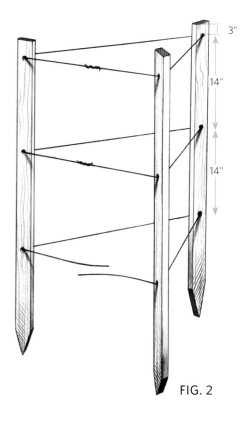

3"

14"

14"

FIG. 2

Horizontal Tomato Support

Left to their own devices, tomato plants sprawl much like squashes do. This frame-style support provides a compromise arrangement between plants and gardener. Once the young seedlings grow up through the wire grid, they are free to spread, but the fruit is kept off the ground.

▼ HORIZONTAL TOMATO SUPPORT. The wire frame of this support keeps the lower plant branches from resting on the soil, where they are more likely to mold or rot.

MATERIALS

Lumber

1"×4" cedar (two 12' lengths)

Supplies

2½'×6' piece of wire fencing
   (with 2"×3" grid)

One box of ¾" galvanized
   poultry staples

Twelve 2" exterior wood
   screws (for the frame)

Eighteen 1¼" exterior wood
   screws (for attaching the
   stakes)

Tools

Tape measure

Pencil

Carpenter's square

Wire cutters

Wood saw

Power drill

⁵⁄₃₂" twist drill bit

Driver bit to match screws

Cutting the lumber. Cut the wood into two 72" lengths for the long sides Ⓐ, two 30" lengths for the short sides Ⓑ, one 30" length for the center stabilizer Ⓒ, and six pointed stakes Ⓓ.

Constructing the support. To create the frame, attach the long sides Ⓐ to the ends of the short sides Ⓑ; attach the center stabilizer Ⓒ as shown in fig. 1. Then staple the wire fencing atop the frame along the perimeter. Flip the frame over, and screw four of the stakes Ⓓ to the inner corners and the remaining two stakes to the long sides Ⓐ on either side of the center stabilizer Ⓒ. Invert the support once again, and set it atop your young plants for them to grow up through.

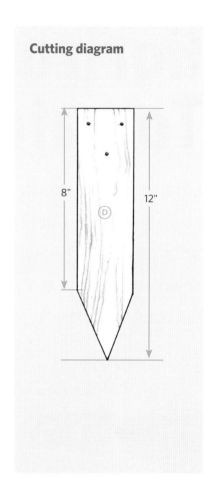

Cutting diagram

FIG. 1

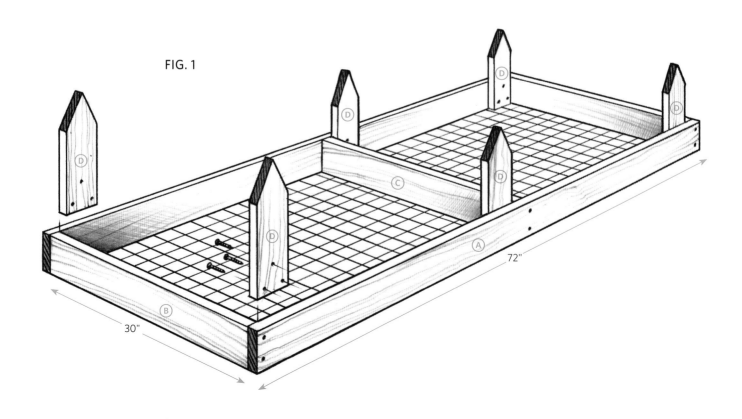

Cylindrical Tomato Cage

Of the many methods of holding and supporting tomatoes, the classic cylinder is a top choice. It's easy to train the vines with this support. And you'll find that picking your ripened tomatoes is a breeze, particularly if you've had to cope with sprawling, earthbound vines before.

▼ CYLINDRICAL TOMATO CAGE. A series of openings cut into the side of this quick-to-assemble cage make it easy to reach in and harvest ripe tomatoes.

MATERIALS

Lumber

Two tomato stakes (4' long)

Supplies

70"×42" piece of wire fencing (with 2"×3" mesh)

Light-gauge wire or twine

Tools

Wire cutters

Pliers

Tape measure

Hammer

Wood saw

Constructing the cage. Shape the wire fencing into a circular cage, overlapping the edges and binding them together with wire or twine. Use wire cutters to cut a number of 6"-square openings in the grid that will allow you to gain access to the plant as it grows.

Installing the cage. Place the cage around the plant. Drive the tomato stakes into the ground on opposite sides of the cage, and fasten the cage to them with wire or twine.

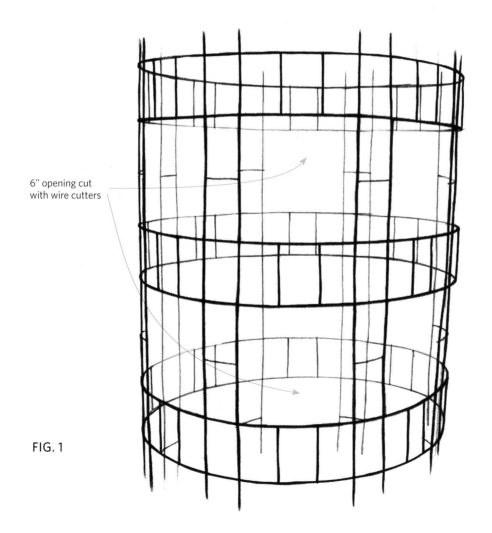

6" opening cut with wire cutters

FIG. 1

A-Frame Bean and Pea Support

Certain plants, such as pole beans and climbing vines, benefit greatly from tall supports. Although you can purchase these supports ready-made, it's fairly easy to construct your own out of hardwood stakes. One option is this A-frame-style support, a basic design that props together a pair of vertical lattice panels.

▼ A-FRAME BEAN AND PEA SUPPORT. The lattice panels of this plant support provide ample height for lofty pole beans and climbing vines.

MATERIALS

Lumber

Thirty-four 1⅛"×1⅛" hard-
   wood birch tomato stakes
   (80" long)

Supplies

2" exterior wood screws
   (80 or so)

Tools

Tape measure
Pencil
Carpenter's square
Wood saw
Power drill
⁵⁄₃₂" twist drill bit
Driver bit to match screws

Cutting the lumber. Leave four stakes full length for the frame sides Ⓐ. For the lattice, leave twelve more full length Ⓑ and cut four others in half Ⓒ. From the remaining stakes, cut two 55" lengths for the frame tops Ⓓ, two 48" lengths for the frame bottoms Ⓔ, two 28" lengths for the long end braces Ⓕ and two 16" lengths for the short end braces Ⓖ.

Constructing the A-frame support. Assemble each of the two A-frame panels by attaching the frame tops Ⓓ and bottoms Ⓔ to the sides Ⓐ. Lay a diagonal pattern of lattice strips Ⓑ & Ⓒ on one side of each panel, predrill the screw holes, and fasten the lattice in place. Trim the ends of the lattice where they extend beyond the frame. Flip over the panels and repeat the process, only this time lay the lattice strips in the opposite direction. Next, lean the tops of the two panels against each other and screw a long brace Ⓕ and a short brace Ⓖ to each side of the A-frame.

Storing your plant support. To store the support between planting seasons, simply remove one screw from each brace and fold the frame flat, tacking the braces to the frame sides until it's time to reassemble it.

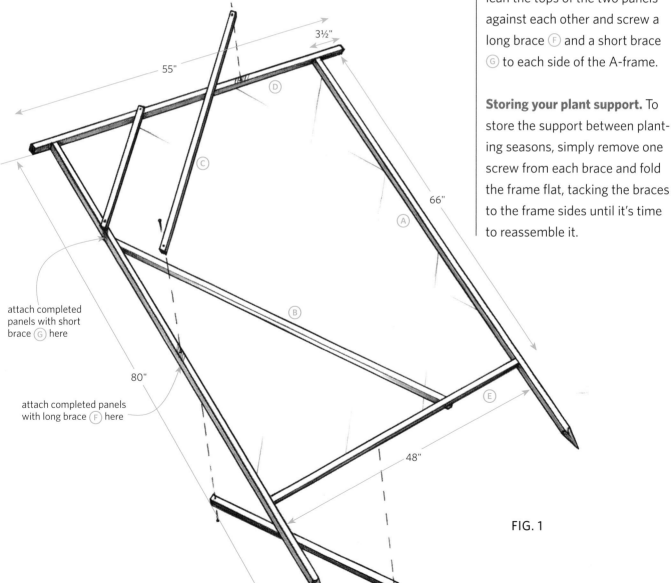

3½"

55"

Ⓓ

Ⓒ

66"

Ⓐ

attach completed
panels with short
brace Ⓖ here

Ⓑ

80"

attach completed panels
with long brace Ⓕ here

Ⓔ

48"

FIG. 1

T-Pea Tower

For climbing plants, such as garden peas and green beans, you can't beat this teepee-style support for simplicity and portability (the bamboo poles make it relatively lightweight). To secure the tower in place, all you need to do is drive a few spikes into the ground and wire or tie the bottom of the poles to them.

▼ T-PEA TOWER. This bamboo plant support is ideal for climbing peas and beans, and it's a snap to erect.

MATERIALS

Lumber
Ten ½" bamboo poles (6' long)

Supplies
¼"-thick rope or wire
Strong rubber band
Ten gutter spikes

Tools
Utility knife
Wire cutter
Hammer

Assembling the t-pea. Choose your garden location. Bundle the bamboo together, and wrap the rubber band around the top of the bundle. Spread the bottom of the bundle to create the perimeter of a teepee, with the poles spaced equally apart.

Hammer the gutter spikes into the ground around the perimeter, each one perpendicular to the end of a pole. Tie or wire the bamboo to the spikes to secure the structure to the ground. Reinforce the rubber band at the top of the teepee with rope or wire.

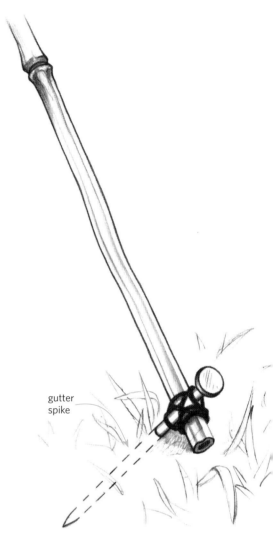

gutter spike

FIG. 1

Teepee Planting Tips

Unlike bush beans, pole beans can grow as tall as 6' to 8' and will benefit greatly from a teepee-style structure to climb. If the poles of your teepee are farther apart than the one featured here, fill the spaces with a zigzag pattern of twine to provide additional climbing surfaces. When planting the seeds, space them about 2" apart around the perimeter of the teepee. As the vines mature, train them to climb the poles, and mulch with straw or grass clippings to help retain soil moisture.

Handy House

Mounted to a post near your garden entrance, this house-style box will come in handy for holding items you may now lug around in your pockets.

▼ HANDY HOUSE. This garden-side storage box keeps planting aids at hand, saving you many return trips to the house or shed.

MATERIALS

Lumber

2"×4" cedar (8' length)

1"×8" cedar (6' length)

1"×10" cedar (6' length)

Supplies

Pair of 1½"×1¼" hinges and screws to go with them

1½" hook-and-eye door latch

2¼" trim-head screws (15 or so)

1⅝" trim-head screws (15 or so)

Small brass hook

Notepad

Two poultry staples

Tools

Tape measure

Pencil

Combination square

Wood saw

Power drill

⅛" twist drill bit

Driver bit to match screws

Shovel

Awl

Phillips screwdriver

Utility knife

¾" chisel

Extension-bit holder

Staple gun

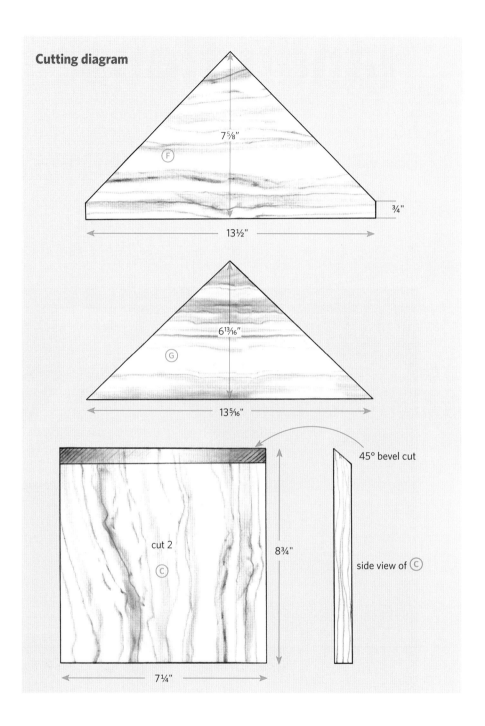

Cutting diagram

7⅝"

F

¾"

13½"

6¹³⁄₁₆"

G

13⁵⁄₁₆"

45° bevel cut

cut 2

C

8¾"

7¼"

side view of C

Moving In

You'll soon find many uses for your handy house, from string for lining up rows to a trowel to supplies you usually have to go back to the house for (a saltshaker for discouraging the cabbage moths, a duster of rotenone, rubber knee pads worn for the fine weeding, a section of old sheeting to be torn up for tomato ties). It's also great for storing a notepad and a pencil to jot down when you planted what and where.

Cutting the lumber. From the 2"×4", cut one 7' length for the post.

From the 1"×8", cut one 13½" length for the back wall Ⓐ, one 12" length for the bottom Ⓑ, and one 12" length for the door Ⓗ. Also cut two 8¾" lengths for the sides Ⓒ, and bevel one end of each length at a 45° angle, as shown in the cutting diagram.

From the 1"×10", cut one 12" length Ⓓ and one 11¼" length Ⓔ for the roof pieces and one 4½"×2¼" length for the chimney cap. Also cut a back gable Ⓕ and a front gable Ⓖ as shown in the cutting diagram.

Constructing the handy house. Start by screwing the sides Ⓒ to the bottom Ⓑ, with the beveled ends at the top. Then attach the back wall Ⓐ and the back gable Ⓕ. For the roof, attach the long piece Ⓓ to the end of the shorter piece Ⓔ (creating an inverted V shape). Position the roof atop the walls, flush with the back of the house. Screw down through the roof into the tops of the side walls Ⓒ and the back gable Ⓕ. (See fig. 1.)

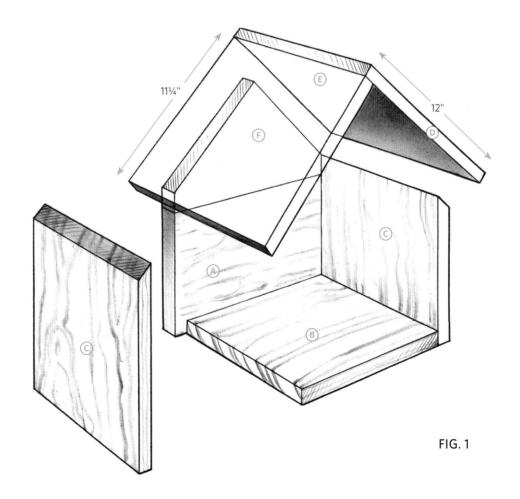

FIG. 1

Use the hinges to attach the door Ⓗ in fig. 2 as shown leaving a 3/32" gap around it. Screw a scrap block of wood inside the house for a doorstop, then install the hook and eye. Fit the front gable Ⓖ in place, and make sure the door swings freely beneath it (if it doesn't, you'll have to trim the gable). Then screw down

through the roof into the top of the gable to secure it.

Screw the chimney cap to the top of the post, and attach the post to the back of the house. Dig a hole in the ground, and set the post to the desired height. Backfill the hole with gravel to provide good drainage.

Screw the brass hook into the inside of the door, and hang the notepad on it. For a pencil holder, tack the two poultry staples to the wood beside the pad, spacing them a few inches apart, one above the other. Tack the upper staple just deep enough to hold it in place (so you can slide the pencil down through it) and set the lower staple deeper, leaving just enough space for the pencil tip to fit through. (See fig. 3.)

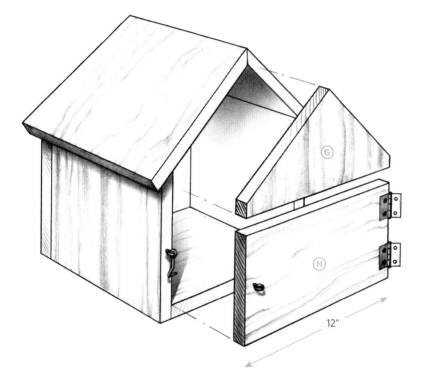

FIG. 2

12"

BUILDER'S TIP

When installing the hinges, hold them in place and use an awl to poke starter holes where the screws will go.

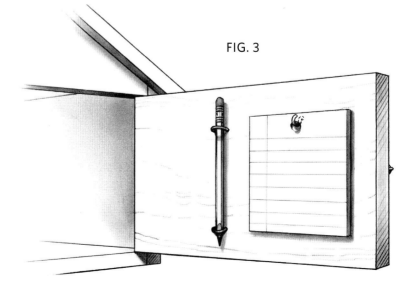

FIG. 3

Tool Rack

MATERIALS

Lumber
1"×4" cedar (two 8' lengths)

Supplies
1⅝" exterior wood screws (20 or so)

2½" mounting screws (8 or so)

Tools
Tape measure

Pencil

Carpenter's square

Wood saw

Power drill

⁵⁄₃₂" twist drill bit

1½" spade drill bit

Driver bit to match screws

You'll find that your gardening chores will be completed much more quickly and you'll be in a better frame of mind if your tools are readily available. When a hunt for a hoe precedes hoeing the peas, the work becomes a chore. There's no better way to avoid such troubles than by creating a place for each tool. This rack features channels in the upper shelf for tool handles to slide into and shallow cups in the bottom shelf to hold them in place.

▲ TOOL RACK. Long-handled tools, such as hoes and shovels, slide handily into the grooves of this wall-mounted rack.

Cutting and drilling the lumber. From the cedar, cut four 42" lengths: one for the top shelf Ⓐ, one for the bottom shelf Ⓑ, and two for the shelf cleats Ⓒ. Also cut four 2¾" lengths for the brackets Ⓓ, with one clipped corner on each. Drill the two shelves as specified in the cutting diagram, going all the way through the wood of the top shelf Ⓐ but just partially through the wood of the bottom shelf to create shallow depressions for the tops of the tool handles to rest in.

Constructing the rack. Fasten each shelf Ⓐ & Ⓑ to a cleat Ⓒ so the pieces are perpendicular, screwing the wood together all along the length. Attach a pair of brackets Ⓓ under each shelf, placing them 2″ in from the ends.

Installing the rack. Use the larger screws to mount the assembled shelves to the wall, spacing the top shelf 40" above the bottom one.

BUILDER'S TIP

To avoid splinter-
ing when drilling
a large hole, use a
spade bit to drill
just until the
point of the bit
breaks the surface
of the opposite
side. Then turn the
board over, place a
block of scrap wood
under the hole, and
finish drilling it
from that side.

Cutting diagram

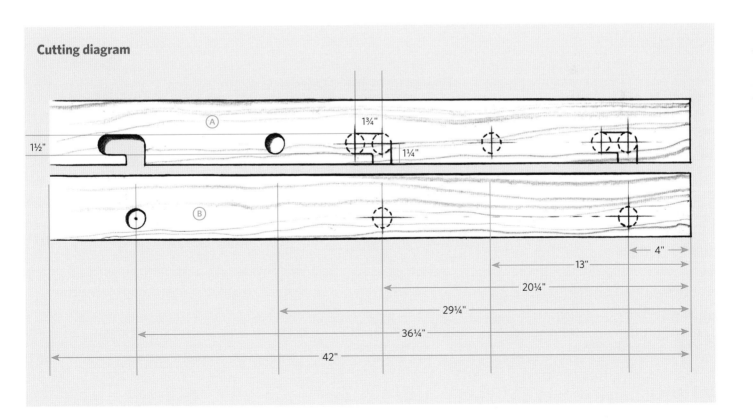

Potting Bench

MATERIALS

Lumber

2"×6" cedar (10' length and four 8' lengths)

2"×4" cedar (10' length and three 8' lengths)

Supplies

2½" decking screws (100 or so)

Tools

Tape measure

Pencil

Carpenter's square

Wood saw

Power drill

⁵⁄₃₂" twist drill bit

Driver bit to match screws

Whether you're repotting that old begonia or shifting a hundred tomato plants from flats to peat pots, a workspace suited to the purpose makes the job a pleasure. Here's a freestanding model that is roomy yet not so wide that it is difficult to reach across. The shelf underneath provides a little storage space (great for those extra clay pots and potting tools).

Beyond the Gardening

As indispensable as this rustic bench is for gardeners, it also serves well in other backyard arenas. Place it near the grill and you have a spacious surface for prepping or serving barbecue fare. If you screw a few hooks into the table ends, you'll have a handy place to hang long-handled spatulas, tongs, and grill forks. Another option is to use the bench as a storage station for your kids' outdoor toys or for lawn-game equipment, such as a croquet set, badminton rackets, horseshoes, and lawn darts.

▲ POTTING BENCH. A spacious work surface and lower storage shelf make this bench invaluable for vegetable and flower gardeners alike.

Cutting the lumber. From the 2"×6", cut six 47¾" lengths for the tabletop Ⓐ and seven 29⅛" lengths for the lower shelf Ⓑ.

From the 2"×4", cut two 45⅜" lengths for the frame front and back Ⓒ, three 29⅛" lengths for the frame sides and center Ⓓ, four 30½" legs Ⓔ, and two 42⅜" lengths for the bottom shelf supports Ⓕ.

Constructing the bench. Make up the frame to support the tabletop by screwing the front and back pieces Ⓒ to opposite ends of the side and center pieces Ⓓ. Next, join each pair of legs Ⓔ by attaching one of the bottom shelf supports Ⓕ, 10" up from the bottom of the legs. Screw the leg tops into the inner corners of the tabletop frame. Finally, fasten the tabletop Ⓐ and lower shelf boards Ⓑ in place.

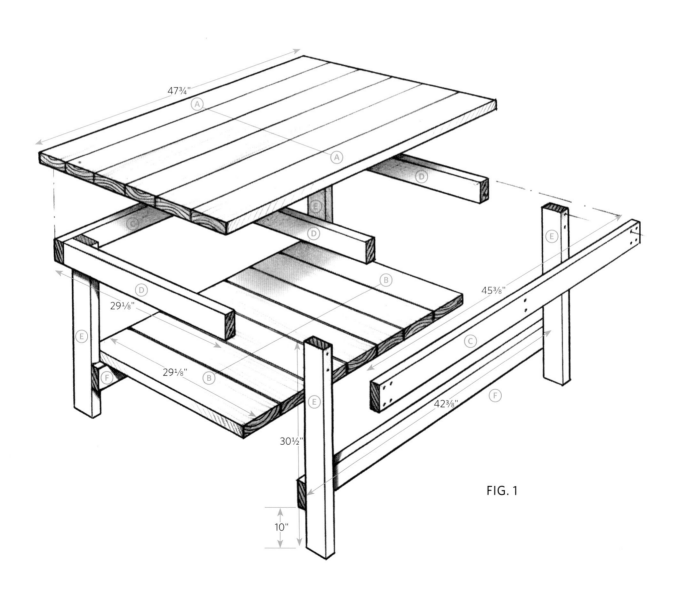

FIG. 1

Lattice Shade Cover

MATERIALS

Lumber

2"×2" cedar balusters (five 36" lengths)

Lattice (20½"×35¾")

Supplies

4d galvanized box nails (30 or so)

Four 2½" screws (for attaching the legs)

Tools

Tape measure

Pencil

Combination square

Wood saw

Power drill

5⁄32" twist drill bit

Driver bit to match screws

If you like to sow lettuce every couple of weeks for season-long harvesting, this shade cover can be a big asset for plantings during the hotter summer months. By filtering the sunlight, the screen helps prevent the lettuce from quickly going to seed and becoming bitter.

▼ LATTICE SHADE COVER. Equipped with collapsible legs, this wooden screen is easy to store when you're not using it.

Cutting the lumber. From the 2"×2", reserve two 36" lengths for the front and back of the cover frame Ⓐ. From the remaining 2"×2", cut two 17¾" lengths for the sides Ⓑ. Also cut four 16¾" lengths for the legs Ⓒ and round the corners (this will keep the leg tops from rubbing on the lattice when you collapse the shade cover for storage at the end of the season).

Constructing the shade cover. Make up the frame by attaching the front and back Ⓐ to the sides Ⓑ. Attach the legs Ⓒ with single screws, as shown in fig. 1, so that they will pivot. Then attach the lattice to the top of the frame.

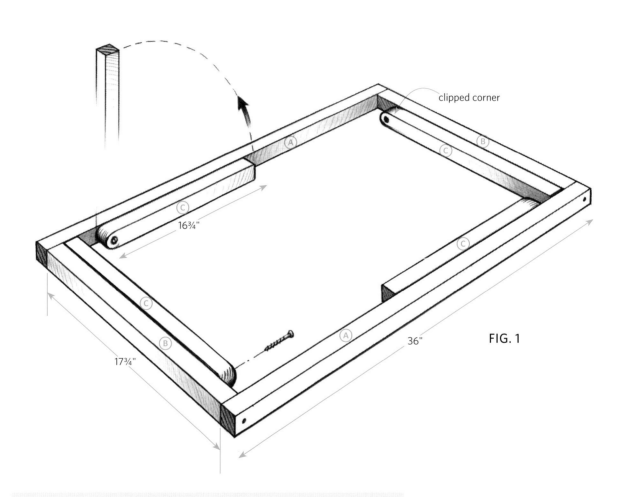

clipped corner

16¾"

17¾"

36"

FIG. 1

Keep It Cool

Not all plants like full sun. Spinach, for example, doesn't germinate well in very warm soils. Placing a shade cover over a planting area a week ahead of time can help moderate the temperature. It's also a good idea to shade the emerging seedlings and young plants during hot spells (above 80°F/27°C) to prevent wilting and bolting. Lettuce, too, should be kept partially shaded when grown in warm weather.

Hanging Planter

MATERIALS

Lumber
1"×6" cedar (4' length)
2"×2" cedar (two 3' lengths)

Supplies
2 medium-size clay pots
   (6" to 7" in diameter)
⅜" rope (three 41" lengths)
Twelve 2" wood screws

Tools
Tape measure
Pencil
Combination square
Wood saw
Jigsaw
Power drill
½" spade drill bit
5/32" twist drill bit
Driver bit to match screws

What's nice about this hanging planter is that the plants can be easily inserted and removed while they're still in their pots, allowing you to exchange them for others without digging out and replacing soil.

Planter Pointers

Besides being a wonderful option for showcasing summer annuals, a hanging planter works well for a variety of vegetables, including vines such as tomatoes and running beans. You can even grow cucumbers and some squashes in one. When choosing a spot, it's wise to avoid places that offer no shelter from the wind, not only because the planter will swing about but also to prevent the plants from drying out. Most importantly, bear in mind that hanging plants can be quite heavy, particularly once you water them. Be sure to buy hooks and brackets designed to bear the actual weight and then some.

▲ HANGING PLANTER. With room for two good-size pots, this planter is especially well suited
   for flowers and herbs.

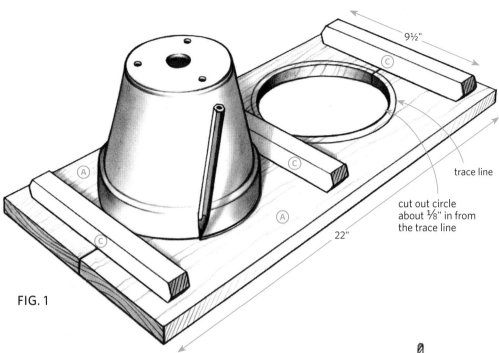

9½"

trace line

cut out circle
about ⅛" in from
the trace line

22"

FIG. 1

Cutting the lumber. From the 1"×6",
cut two 22" lengths for the platform
Ⓐ. From the 2"×2", cut a 22" length
for a spreader bar Ⓑ. Also cut three
9½" lengths for battens Ⓒ, and
bevel the edges.

Constructing the planter. Set up the
pieces as shown in fig. 1, and trace
around the pots. Cut out the circles
about ⅛" inside the tracings.

Reassemble the pieces, and screw
the battens Ⓒ in place. Then drill
½" holes for the rope in the ends of
the side battens Ⓒ and through the
platform boards Ⓐ. Drill ½" rope
holes through the top and sides of
the spreader bar Ⓑ at both ends,
and thread the rope lengths through
them (fig. 2).

Knot the ropes to keep them from
slipping back through the holes.

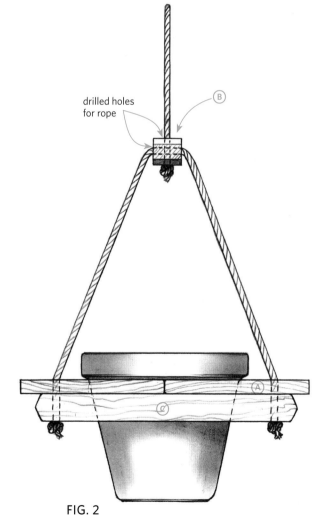

drilled holes
for rope

Ⓑ

FIG. 2

Window Box Planter

It's amazing how much a window box of colorful flowers can dress up a house. This planter at the kitchen window features edible flowers (calendula and Johnny-jump-ups) along with favorite herbs (cilantro, purple basil, sages, and oregano), close at hand for last-minute additions to summer meals.

▼ WINDOW BOX PLANTER. This window planter is decorative yet easy to construct and install.

MATERIALS

Lumber

1"×6" cedar (12' length)

Supplies

Eighteen 2¼" exterior
   trim-head screws
Six 4d galvanized box nails
Four 2½" exterior #8
   pan-head screws for
   mounting

Tools

Tape measure
Pencil
Carpenter's square
Wood saw
Jigsaw
Power drill
⅛" twist drill bit for predrilling trim-head screw
   holes
⅜" twist drill bit for
   drilling drainage holes
Driver bit to match
   trim-head screws
Driver bit or screwdriver to
   match pan-head screws
Compass or paint can for
   drawing curves

Cutting the lumber. From the 1"×6", cut two 30" lengths for the front and upper back Ⓐ. Cut one 30" length for the lower back Ⓑ and cut the decorative bottom as indicated in the cutting diagram. Cut one 28½" length for the bottom Ⓒ. Cut two 11" lengths for the sides Ⓓ, and cut the decorative bottom as indicated in the cutting diagram. From scrap wood removed from piece Ⓑ, cut one 23¾" length for the trim Ⓔ, and cut the decoration as indicated. (See the builder's tip on page 68 for advice on cutting the decorations.)

Cutting diagram

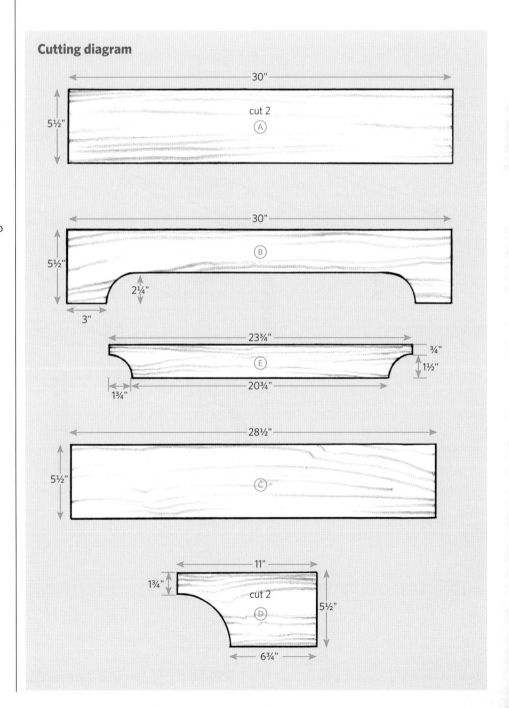

Constructing the planter. Attach the trim Ⓔ to the front of the planter Ⓐ by nailing through the back side of the front board into the trim. Then attach the front and upper back boards Ⓐ to the sides Ⓓ. Drill randomly spaced drainage holes in the bottom board Ⓒ; then fit the board in place so it is flush with the lower edges of the front and back, and screw it in place. Screw the lower back board Ⓑ in place.

BUILDER'S TIP

To create the curved cutting lines, simply trace around paint cans (a gallon size for the side boards Ⓓ and a quart size for the lower back Ⓑ and the decorative front trim board Ⓔ).

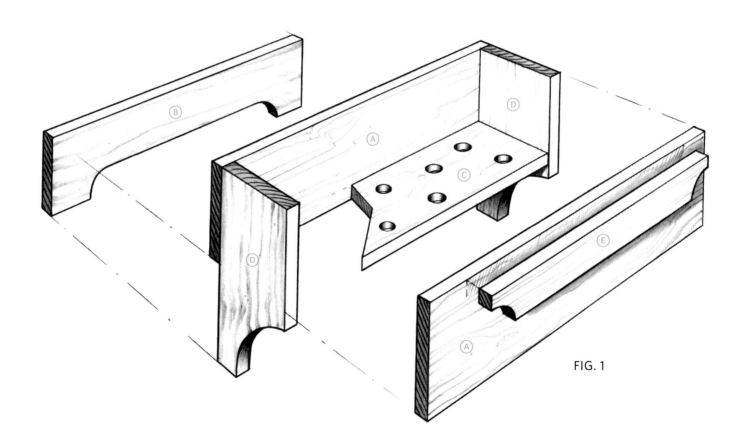

FIG. 1

Square Planter

MATERIALS

Lumber

2"×2" cedar balusters
(ten 3' lengths)

1"×4" cedar (six 8' lengths)

Supplies

2½" pan-head exterior
screws (40 or so)

1⅝" exterior wood screws
(120 or so)

Landscaping cloth to line
the finished planter

Tools

Tape measure

Pencil

Carpenter's square

Wood saw

Jigsaw

Power drill

5/32" twist drill bit

Driver bit to match screws

Like other gardening containers, this square planter can be stationed where you choose to do your gardening. Its depth is one of its top selling points. You can fill it with plenty of soil, which means your vegetables or flowers will naturally stay fresh longer. While the design is a basic box, the contoured trim boards at its base lend the planter a decorative flair.

BUILDER'S TIP

When screwing the wood together, use 2½" screws for the 2" material and 1⅝" screws for the 1" material. Space the balusters 3" in from the corner posts and 3" apart from each other.

▲ SQUARE PLANTER. Filled with produce or flowers, this planter makes an attractive focal point in a yard or set along a driveway.

Cutting the lumber. From the balusters, cut four 17¾" posts Ⓐ, eight 16½" rails Ⓑ, and twelve 11¾" balusters Ⓒ.

From the 1"×4", cut sixteen 14⅝" boards for the inner walls Ⓓ, four 19¼" floorboards Ⓔ, and four 18" top trim boards Ⓕ. You'll also need to cut four base trim boards Ⓖ, as specified in the cutting diagram.

Constructing the planter. Assemble each of the four wall sections with one post Ⓐ on the end, then fasten the walls together to create the planter frame, as shown in fig. 1.

Cutting diagram

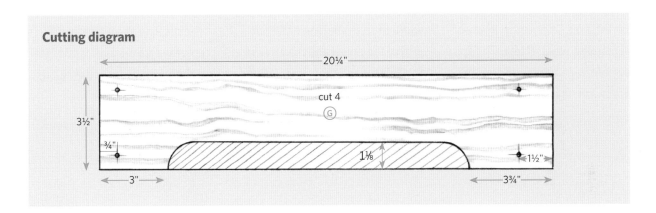

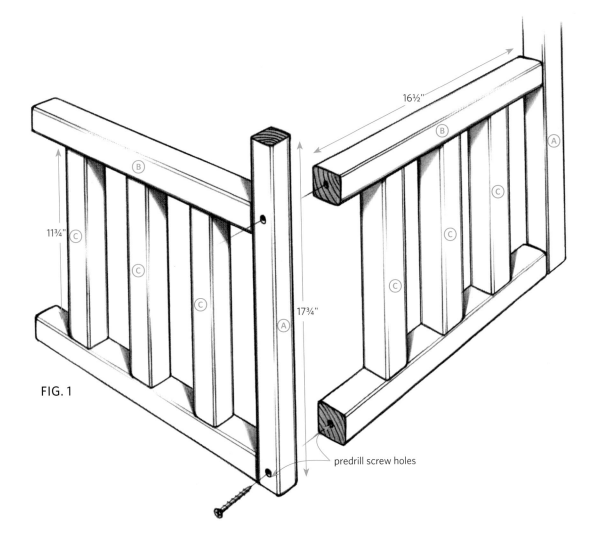

FIG. 1

predrill screw holes

Next, attach the inner wall boards Ⓓ (see fig. 2). To do this, fit a board into each of the two corners of one wall, then use two more boards to cover the openings between the balusters. Repeat the process on the opposite wall, mirroring the boards on the first. Then finish the two remaining walls. (Note: The spacing between the boards on these walls will be a little tighter.)

Next, attach the floor boards Ⓔ to the frame, spacing them ¼" apart for drainage.

Attach the first piece of base trim Ⓖ by flushing up the left side with a left corner post (the opposite end will overhang the right corner post) and leaving a pencil's width of space between the bottom of the board and the ground to allow for drainage. Repeat the process to attach the remaining three base trim boards.

Attach the top trim Ⓕ, positioning the boards to form a square, with an inch of overhang along the outer perimeter of the planter frame. Keep in mind that you may have to angle the screws slightly to avoid the corner post screws below.

Finally, line the inside of the planter with a piece of landscaping cloth to help keep the soil in place.

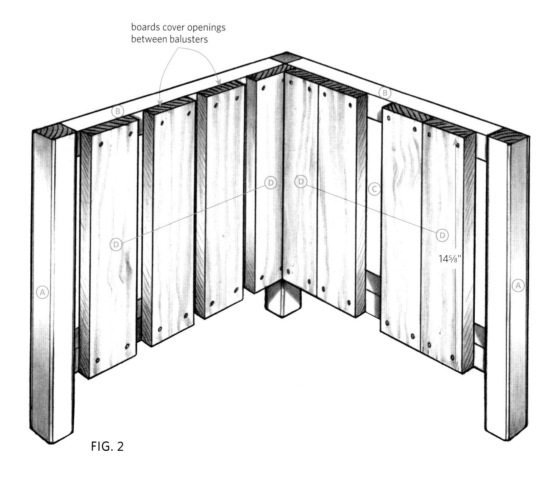

boards cover openings
between balusters

14⅝"

FIG. 2

Welcoming Arbor

MATERIALS

Lumber

2"×6" cedar (12' length)

2"×4" cedar (four 10' lengths)

2"×2" cedar (seven 3' lengths)

1"×6" cedar (two 10' lengths)

1"×4" cedar (four 8' lengths)

Supplies

Twenty 2¼" stainless steel #1 trim-head screws

Eighty-eight 1¼" #6 stainless steel Phillips pan-head screws

Thirty-eight 2½" #8 stainless steel pan-head screws

Tools

Tape measure

Pencil

Combination square

Table saw or circular saw with rip fence

Jigsaw

Power drill

⅛" twist drill bit

#1 square driver bit to match trim-head screws

Phillips driver bit to match pan-head screws

Level for installing

This classic fixture can greatly enhance the visual appeal of a garden. Although often referred to as a "rose arbor," this sturdy structure is equally useful for supporting heavy vegetable vines, such as Italian trombone squash, cucumbers, or cheerful scarlet runner beans.

▲ WELCOMING ARBOR. Homemade lattice panels, curved brackets, and a
ladder-style top make this arbor both ornate and sturdy.

Cutting the lumber. From the 2"×6", cut two rafters Ⓐ, as specified in the cutting diagram.

From the 2"×4", cut four 98½" corner posts Ⓑ (18" will be buried in the ground). Also cut four 18" angled corner brackets Ⓒ, as specified in the cutting diagram.

From the 2"×2", cut seven 36" purlins Ⓓ.

From the 1"×6", cut two 24" roof trim boards Ⓔ and eight 21" arched wall trim boards Ⓕ (once you cut one, you can use it as a template for the others).

Rip all of the 1"×4" in half, then use the pieces to cut four 65½" lengths Ⓖ and four 68" lengths Ⓗ for vertical lattice and eight 21" lengths for horizontal lattice Ⓘ. Mark the long vertical lattice as shown in the cutting diagram. (You'll use this later for attaching the horizontal lattice.)

Cutting diagram

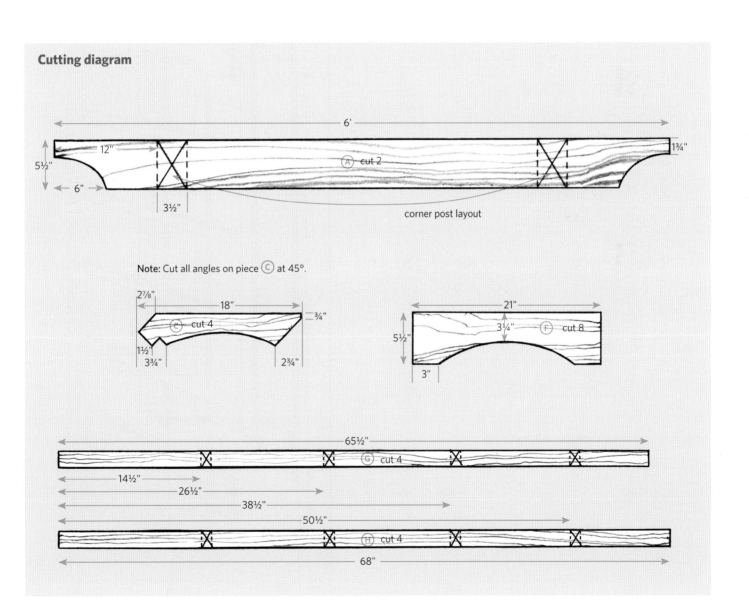

Constructing the arbor. Start by making up two lattice wall panels. For each, first attach a longer vertical lattice Ⓗ to each corner post Ⓑ as shown in fig. 1 (Make sure the layout marks are facing each other.)

Fasten the two corner posts together by attaching arched trim boards Ⓕ at the top and bottom. Then flip the panel over, and attach two shorter vertical lattice Ⓖ to the trim boards Ⓕ, spacing them equally apart, and cover the ends with another pair of arched trim boards Ⓕ. Attach four horizontal lattice Ⓘ, then attach the top roof trim boards Ⓔ to the tops of the corner posts Ⓑ, as shown in fig. 2.

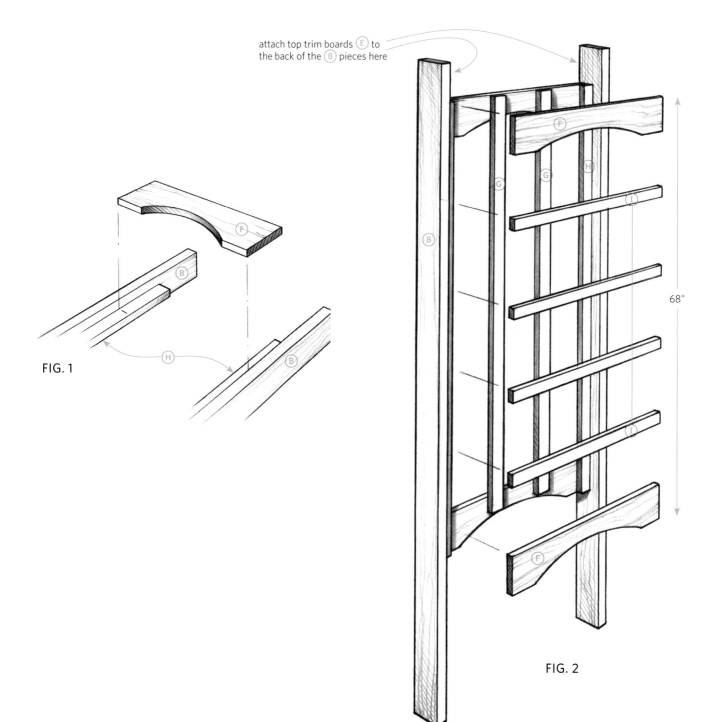

attach top trim boards Ⓔ to the back of the Ⓑ pieces here

FIG. 1

FIG. 2

68"

Assemble the arbor roof as shown in fig. 3. Flip the roof over, and insert the tops of the wall panels 12" in from the ends. Screw through the corner posts into the rafters, making sure they are squared up. Attach the angled brackets to the roof rafters and corner posts, positioning the bottom of the brackets 16" down from the top of the corner posts.

Installing the arbor. Set the corner posts 18" into the ground, and backfill the holes with gravel to provide drainage.

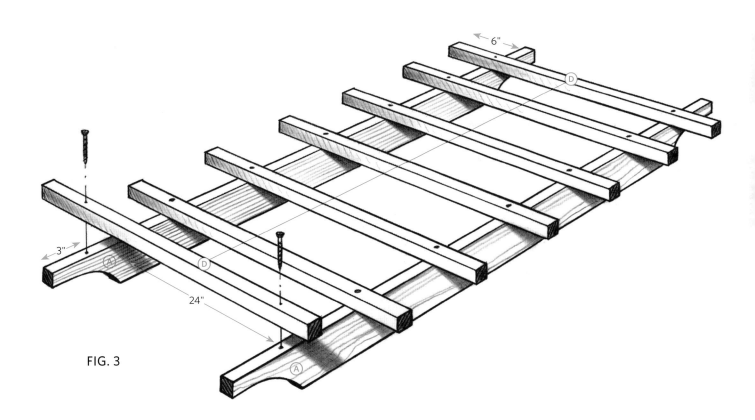

FIG. 3

Garden Gate

MATERIALS

Lumber

1"×6" cedar (10' length and 12' length)

Supplies

4d galvanized box nails

Pair of rustproof gate hinges with mounting screws to attach to a post or fence rail

Tools

Tape measure

Pencil

Carpenter's square

Wood saw

Jigsaw

Framing square

Hammer

Four 3" spring clamps

When building a garden gate, there are a number of things you'll want to consider. It should be wide enough for garden equipment to fit through, close enough to the ground to bar entrance to unwanted animals, and sturdy enough to endure the inevitable — a bump with a cart or a child swinging on it, for instance. And if your garden is on a slope, be certain to install the gate so it opens downhill.

BUILDER'S TIPS

Once you've rounded the center picket, you can use it as a template for the others by simply tracing around it. When attaching the pickets to the rails, angle the nailing pattern to keep the wood from splitting.

▲ GARDEN GATE. Pickets cut to different lengths form a decorative arched top on this cedar gate.

Cutting the lumber. From the 1"×6", cut two 35¾" lengths for the top and bottom rails Ⓐ and a 34" length for a brace Ⓑ. For the pickets, cut four 33½" lengths and rip them to 2¼" wide. Round the top of one 33½" length to use as the center picket Ⓒ. From the remaining lengths, cut two 33⅛" lengths Ⓓ, two 32³⁄₁₆" lengths Ⓔ, and two 30½" lengths Ⓕ, rounding the tops on all of them.

Constructing the gate. Clamp the rails Ⓐ to your work surface so that they are parallel to one another and spaced 14" apart. Measure from corner to corner to make sure they are square. Arrange the pickets Ⓓ, Ⓔ, and Ⓕ atop the rails, as shown in fig. 1, and nail them in place.

Flip the gate over, and place the brace Ⓑ diagonally between the rails. Pencil lines where you need to trim the board so it will fit into place. Nail the trimmed board to the pickets. (See fig. 2.)

Installing the gate. Hang the gate on a sturdy post set 3' into the ground. Use rustproof hardware, and position the gate in such a way that the space between it and the ground does not permit entrance of the very animals you are trying to exclude.

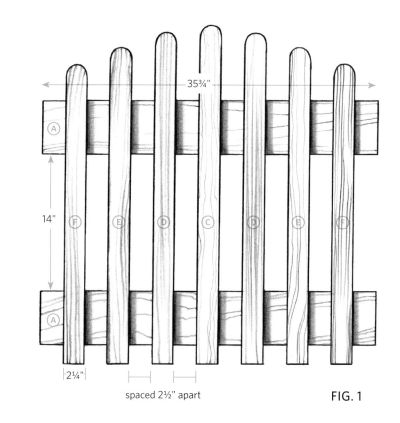

FIG. 1

FIG. 2

Gate Latch

MATERIALS

Lumber

1"×4" (4' length)

⅝" dowel (2½" length)

Supplies

Twelve 4d galvanized box nails

Twelve 6d galvanized box nails

1¼" galvanized wood screw

Tools

Tape measure

Pencil

Carpenter's square

Combination square

Wood saw

Wood file

Power drill

⅝" spade drill bit

Driver bit to match screw

Hammer

Screwdriver to match the wood screw

Wood glue

You can purchase gate latches at your hardware store, but it's easy to build one that will be far more decorative, and sturdier, as well. Here is a simple assembly made of wood that is designed to attach to the top rail of a gate and the adjacent fence section.

▼ GATE LATCH. With little more than a few pieces of scrap wood, you can make a latch that's functional and fun to use.

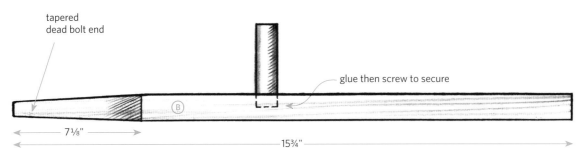

tapered
dead bolt end

glue then screw to secure

B

7⅛"

15¾"

FIG. 1

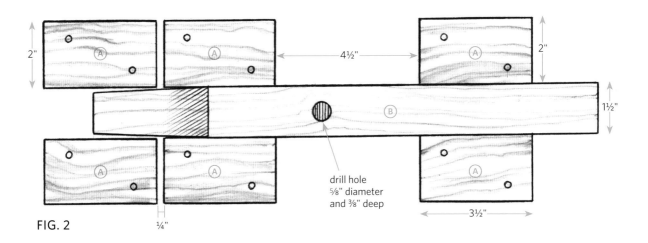

2"

A

A

4½"

A

2"

B

1½"

drill hole
⅝" diameter
and ⅜" deep

A

A

A

3½"

FIG. 2

¼"

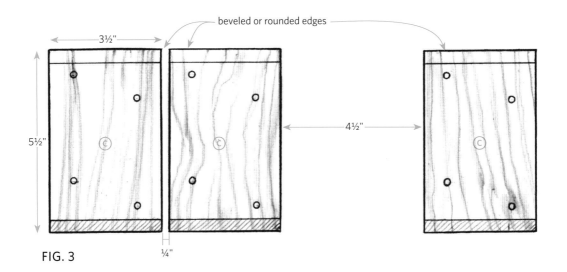

beveled or rounded edges

3½"

C

C

4½"

C

5½"

FIG. 3

¼"

Cutting the lumber. From the 1"×4", cut six 2" lengths for the inside latch blocks Ⓐ; one 15¾"×1½" length for the sliding dead bolt Ⓑ; and three 5½" lengths for the outside latch blocks Ⓒ. Bevel the ends as specified in fig. 3.

Installing the latch. First, attach the dowel, which is the knob on the sliding dead bolt Ⓑ by gluing it into the hole. Then secure it by screwing through the underside of the dead bolt into the bottom of the dowel. (See side view of dead bolt in fig. 1.)

When the glue has dried, attach the inside latch blocks Ⓐ to the gate and fence rail with 4d box nails (fig. 2). Then fasten the outside latch blocks Ⓒ atop the first with 6d box nails so that the dead bolt can slide back and forth but will not fall out (figs. 3 and 4).

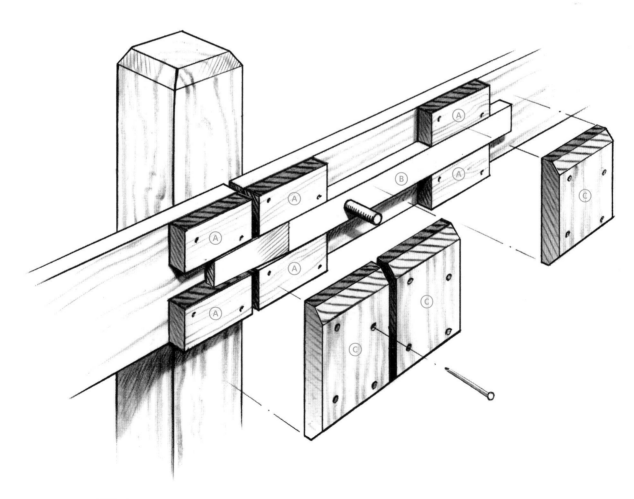

FIG. 4

2 | BUILDING PROJECTS FOR
HARVESTING
AND
PRESERVING

Berry Box

If you're a berry picker, here's a handy carrier that will help keep those fragile raspberries or strawberries from being crushed. It holds six quart cartons and is both sturdy and lightweight. You'll find it useful around the vegetable garden, too, when picking other small produce.

▼ BERRY BOX. A section cut from a broom handle makes for a sturdy grip on this harvest helper.

MATERIALS

Lumber

1"×3" cedar (8' length)
½" exterior plywood
   (18"×12½" piece)
Broomstick (18" length)

Supplies

Ten 6d box nails
Eighteen 4d box nails

Tools

Tape measure
Pencil
Carpenter's square
Wood saw
Hammer
Power drill
⁵⁄₃₂" twist drill bit

Cutting the lumber. From the 1"×3", cut two 16½" lengths for the front and back boards Ⓐ and two 12½" lengths for the sides Ⓑ. Then cut two 13" lengths for handle extensions Ⓒ, and trim the upper corners at an angle.

Constructing the box. Create the box frame by attaching the sides Ⓑ to the ends of the front and back boards Ⓐ. Then nail the plywood Ⓓ to the bottom. Next, attach the handle extensions Ⓒ to the box sides Ⓑ, and nail the broomstick length Ⓔ in place between them.

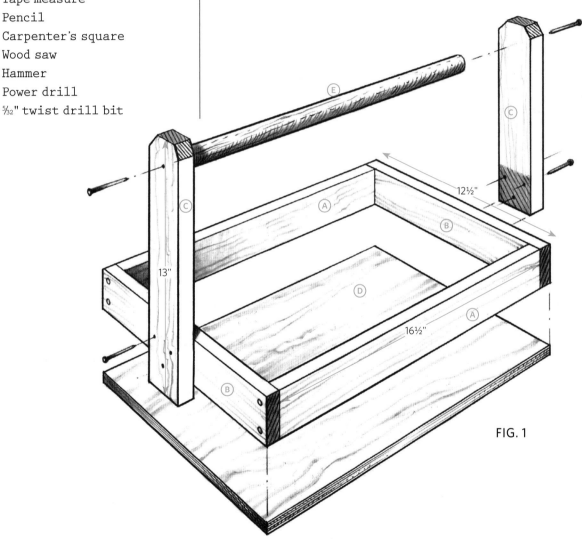

FIG. 1

BUILDER'S TIP

Predrilling screw holes into the center of the broomstick ends will prevent the handle from splitting when you fasten it to the box.

Solar Dryer

MATERIALS

Lumber
1"×6" cedar (6' length)
1"×4" cedar (three 12' lengths)
2"×4" cedar (12' length)
Old window sash (31½" square)

Supplies
Window screening (cut to 31½" square)
Staples to fit staple gun
One pound 6d box nails

Tools
Tape measure
Pencil
Carpenter's square
Wood saw
Hammer
Utility knife (to cut the screening)
Staple gun

In warm, sunny climates, the use of the sun for drying food is practical and inexpensive. Even in less favorable climates, it is often possible to do much of the drying in the sun, then complete the process by placing materials in an oven set at very low heat and with the door left ajar. Here's a dryer that can be used for fruits and vegetables and is fairly simple to build and easy to use. The plan calls for a 31½"-square window sash; if you choose to use another size, you'll have to modify the directions accordingly.

▲ SOLAR DRYER. The top of this homemade dehydrator is a recycled window sash set at an angle to catch the most direct rays from the sun.

Cutting the lumber. From the 1"×6", cut two 31½" lengths for the front and back of the sash frame Ⓐ.

From the 1"×4", cut two 31½" lengths for the sides of the sash frame Ⓑ, six 33" lengths (four for the sides of the stand Ⓒ and two for the sloped boards that go at the top of the stand Ⓓ), and four 34¾" lengths for the front and back of the stand Ⓔ.

From the 2"×4", cut two 25" lengths for the front legs Ⓕ and two 35" lengths for the back legs Ⓖ.

Constructing the dryer. First, make up the sash frame by nailing the front and back pieces Ⓐ to the ends of the sides Ⓑ, flushing up the bottoms. Then staple the screening to the bottom of the frame. (See fig. 1.)

Next, make up each of the two stand sides by nailing the side pieces Ⓒ to the front and back legs Ⓕ & Ⓖ. Attach the sloped boards Ⓓ to the inner sides (fig. 2). Join the two sides by attaching the front and back frame boards Ⓔ to the legs.

Finally, register the sash frame on the stand, then fit the sash within the frame.

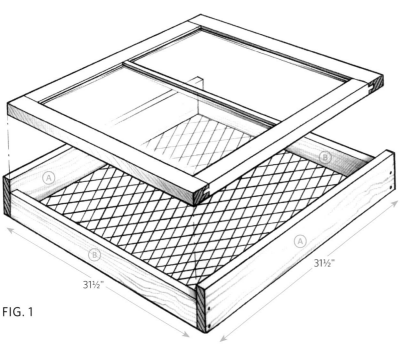

FIG. 1

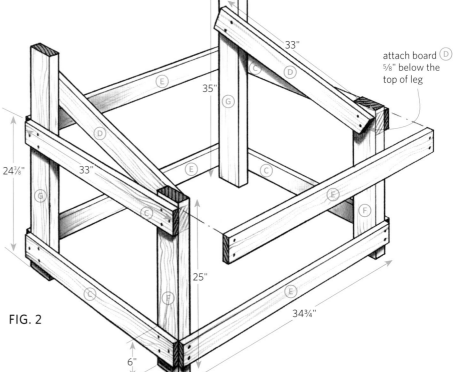

FIG. 2

Outdoor Storage Bin

In cooler climates, storing food outdoors can save a lot of space. The trick is outsmarting the rodents. Here's a storage box that will halt the advances of unwanted pests. It is built with a light wooden frame, is lined with Styrofoam, and features an exterior protective covering of hardware cloth. When it's filled, cover the box with a deep layer of hay or some other insulating material, or sink it into the ground.

▼ OUTDOOR STORAGE BIN. Hardware cloth stapled to the exterior makes this insulated storage box pestproof.

MATERIALS

Lumber

1"×10" cedar (14' length)

1"×4" cedar (three 12' lengths)

2"×4" cedar (8' length)

Supplies

1" foam insulation (three 2'×8' sheets)

Two 5½" sturdy exterior handles/pulls with mounting screws

One pound 6d galvanized box nails

One pound 4d galvanized box nails

1¼" fender washers (60 or so)

One pound 2" exterior Phillips-head wood screws

Twenty-four 1½" exterior Phillips-head wood screws (for fastening the foam to the inside of the rails)

½" hardware cloth (two 5' rolls)

One pound ¾" poultry staples

Tools

Tape measure

Pencil

Carpenter's square

Wood saw

Utility knife (for cutting the foam)

Hammer

Power drill

⁵⁄₃₂" twist drill bit

Driver bit to match screws

Phillips screwdriver

Staple gun

Tin snips

Work gloves

Cutting the lumber and the foam insulation. Cut the 1"×10" into three 51¾" cover boards Ⓐ.

From the 1"×4", cut three 27¾" cover battens Ⓑ, four 47½" top and bottom rails for the front and back of the bin Ⓒ, and four 25" top and bottom rails for the sides of the bin Ⓓ.

Cut the 2"×4" into six 12" rail supports Ⓔ.

From the foam cut two 23½"×47½" rectangles Ⓕ for the top and bottom of the bin, and reserve the rest for cutting to fit between the bin framing.

Constructing the bin. Begin by constructing the bin box frame and cover, as shown in fig. 1. Using 2" screws and fender washers, fasten one of the cut foam pieces Ⓕ to the underside of the cover and the other to the rail supports Ⓔ on the bottom of the box frame. (See fig. 2.)

Now cut the rest of the foam to fit between the rails Ⓓ & Ⓒ on the outside of the box Ⓖ and between the rail supports Ⓔ on the inside of the box Ⓗ. Attach these pieces to the rails and supports with 1½" screws and fender washers as shown in fig. 2.

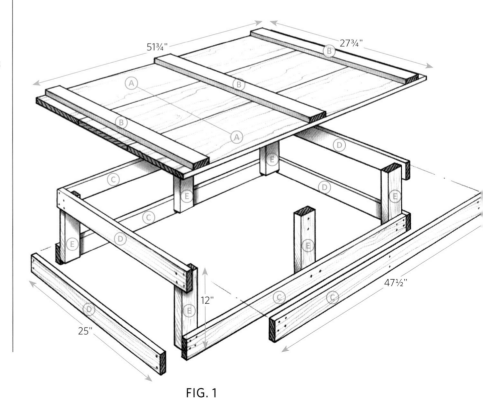

FIG. 1

To protect the contents of the bin from animals, wrap the outside of the bin with hardware cloth and staple it in place. Finally, fasten the handles to the battens on the top of the cover, and the bin is ready to use.

BUILDER'S TIPS

To make sure the bin's box frame is square, first tack the corners and check them with a framing square before driving in the nails all the way. When constructing the cover, nail through the cover boards into the battens, angling the nails slightly to keep them from poking through the other side.

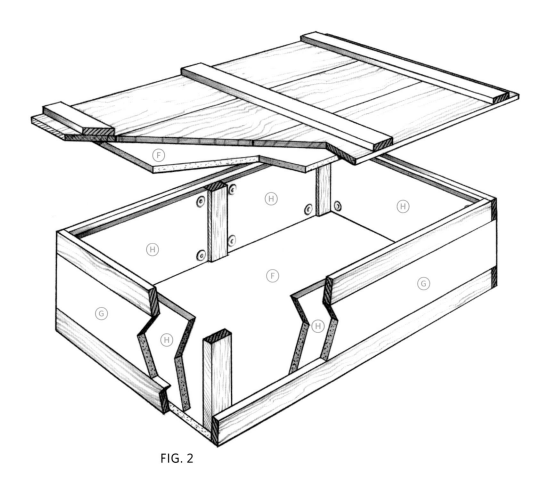

FIG. 2

Garden Bench

MATERIALS

Lumber

2"×8" cedar (two 8' lengths)

2"×4" cedar (6' length)

1"×4" cedar (10' length and 12' length)

Supplies

3" exterior wood screws (26 or so)

2" exterior wood screws (50 or so)

Tools

Tape measure

Pencil

Speed square

Wood saw

Power drill

⅛" twist drill bit

Driver bit to match screws

80-grit sandpaper

Every garden needs a bench, whether it's simply a place to set your trowel and other hand tools (so you won't waste time looking for them minutes later) or a holding spot for a bucket of peas, a pile of fat squashes, or bunches of carrots. Even better, it provides a great seat, after hours of work, for reflecting on the wonders of gardening.

A Simple Seat and Sturdy Stand

Of the many different styles of garden seating you can choose from, the classic backless bench is arguably the most versatile. Besides being portable, it allows you to sit facing whichever direction you like and can be placed at the end of a picnic table to provide additional seating for outdoor gatherings. It also comes in handy for container gardening. Instead of placing pots directly on the ground, you can set them on benches, where they will drain well.

▲ GARDEN BENCH. Basic wood cuts and simple joinery make this solid garden seat a cinch to assemble.

Cutting diagram

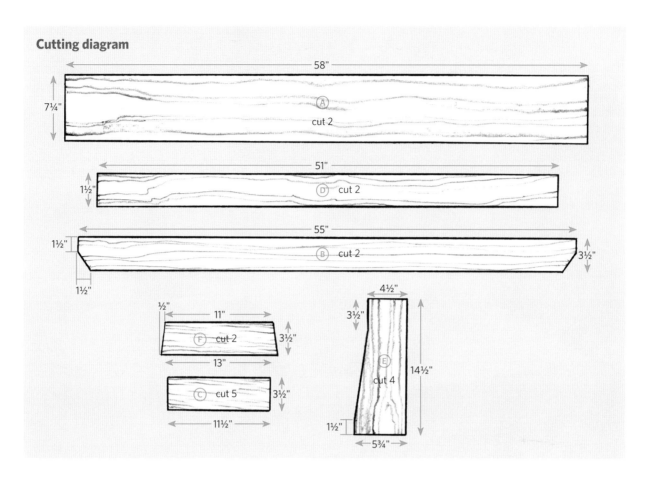

Cutting the lumber. From the 2"×8", cut two 58" lengths for the seat Ⓐ and four 14½" lengths for the legs Ⓔ, trimmed as shown in the cutting diagram. From the 2"×4", cut five 11½" lengths for the blocks Ⓒ; from the 1"×4", cut two 55" lengths for the top rails Ⓑ; two 51" lengths for the bottom rails Ⓓ; and two 13" lengths for the leg battens Ⓕ, trimmed as shown in the cutting diagram.

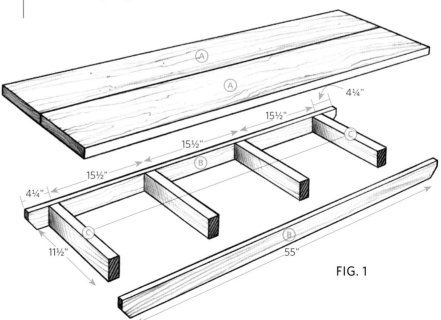

FIG. 1

Constructing the bench. Make up the frame for the seat by attaching the two top rails Ⓑ to the seat blocks Ⓒ. Center the two seat boards Ⓐ atop the frame, and fasten them to the tops of the blocks. Flip the seat assembly over. (See fig. 1.)

Next, make up each of the two leg assemblies. Attach a bottom rail Ⓓ to each pair of legs Ⓔ, 1½" from the bottom, as shown in fig. 2. Fasten the tops of the legs to the outside of the end seat blocks. (See fig. 3.) Reinforce the connection by screwing through

the face of the upper rails into the legs as well.

Finally, connect the two leg assemblies with a leg batten on each end Ⓕ and a block Ⓒ inserted between the centers of the bottom rails. Round all the edges with sandpaper.

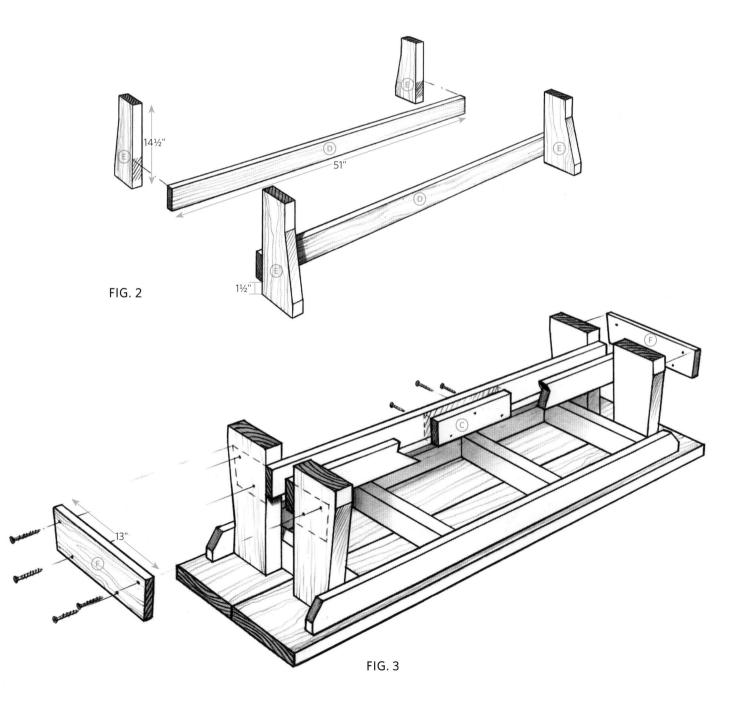

FIG. 2

FIG. 3

Handy Lightweight Bench

MATERIALS

Lumber
1"×12" mahogany (8' length)

Supplies
Eighteen 2¼" stainless steel trim-head screws

Four 1⅝" stainless steel trim-head screws

Tools
Tape measure

Pencil

Carpenter's square

Wood saw

Jigsaw

Power drill

⅛" twist drill bit

⅜" spade drill bit

Driver bit to match screws

With a handhold cut right into the edge of the seat, this lightweight bench is easy to tote around to different sections of the garden. When constructing it, drawing the curved cutting lines is handily done by tracing around a CD. Just be sure to double-check your measurements; they need to be precise for the pieces to screw together properly.

BUILDER'S TIP

When predrilling the screw holes, use a ⅛" drill bit. Then fasten all the pieces with 2¼" trim-head screws — but use 1⅝" screws for the four seat corners to avoid hitting the screws in the apron boards.

▲ HANDY LIGHTWEIGHT BENCH. Constructed of exterior-grade mahogany,
  this durable bench will last through many gardening seasons.

Cutting the lumber. From the 1"×12", cut two 29" lengths for the aprons Ⓐ, one 30" length for the seat Ⓑ, and two 17¼" lengths for the legs Ⓒ. Use an old CD as a template to cut the openings for the handholds in the seat and aprons and the shaping at the bottom of the legs, as shown in the cutting diagram.

Cutting diagram

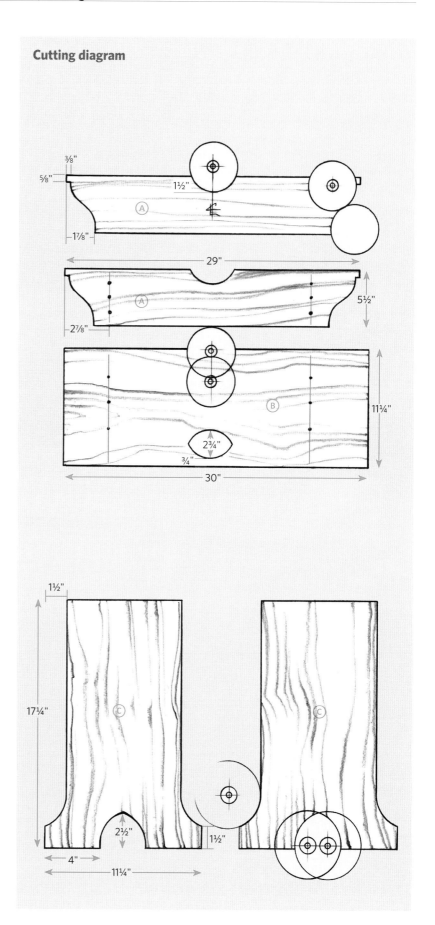

Constructing the bench. Connect the legs Ⓒ by attaching the aprons Ⓐ on either side (there should be a 2½" overhang on each end). Next, center the seat Ⓑ atop the leg assembly, and fasten it to the tops of the legs and aprons. (See fig. 1.)

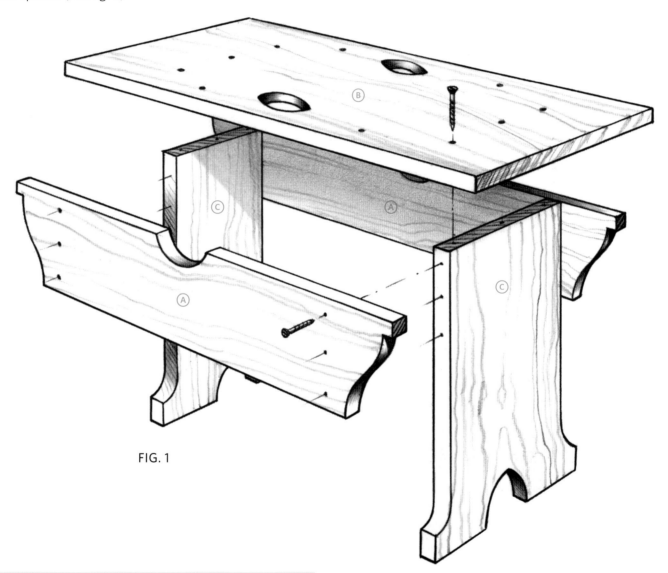

FIG. 1

BUILDER'S TIP

When creating the handhold in the seat, use a ⅜" bit to drill a starter hole for the jigsaw blade.

3

BUILDING PROJECTS FOR

RELAXING
AND
ENJOYING
YOUR BACKYARD

Picnic Table

MATERIALS

Lumber

2"×6" cedar (seven 12' lengths)

2"×4" cedar (10' length and 8' length)

Supplies

2½" exterior pan-head decking screws (120 or so)

Eight 3"×⅜" exterior carriage bolts with washers and nuts

Tools

Tape measure

Pencil

Large carpenter's square

Wood saw

Power drill

5/32" drill bit

⅜" spade drill bit

⅞" spade drill bit

Driver bit to match screws

Ratchet and socket to fit carriage bolt nut

Wood file

80-grit sandpaper

There's nothing more pleasant than dining outdoors in the shade of a tree on a hot summer day. And there's nothing more convenient than having a picnic table set up and ready to use in that very spot. This classic version features attached benches and ample eating space for the whole family. Of course, it won't take long to realize that a picnic table provides much more than reserved seating for a homegrown feast. It's a great recreational prop for spending more time outdoors, perhaps working on arts and crafts that are too messy to complete indoors, or simply playing a favorite board game on a lazy summer afternoon.

▲ PICNIC TABLE. This spacious outdoor table offers prime seating for feasting on your garden harvest.

Cutting the lumber. From the 2"×6", cut nine 71½" lengths (five for the tabletop and four for the seats) Ⓐ, two 54" lengths for the seat supports Ⓑ, and four 36" lengths for the legs Ⓒ.

From the 2"×4", cut two 28½" lengths for the inner battens Ⓓ, two 28½" lengths for the outer battens Ⓔ, two 21" lengths with 40° angle cuts on both ends for angle braces Ⓕ, and four 11¼" lengths for the seat battens Ⓖ. Trim the pieces as shown in the cutting diagram.

Cutting diagram

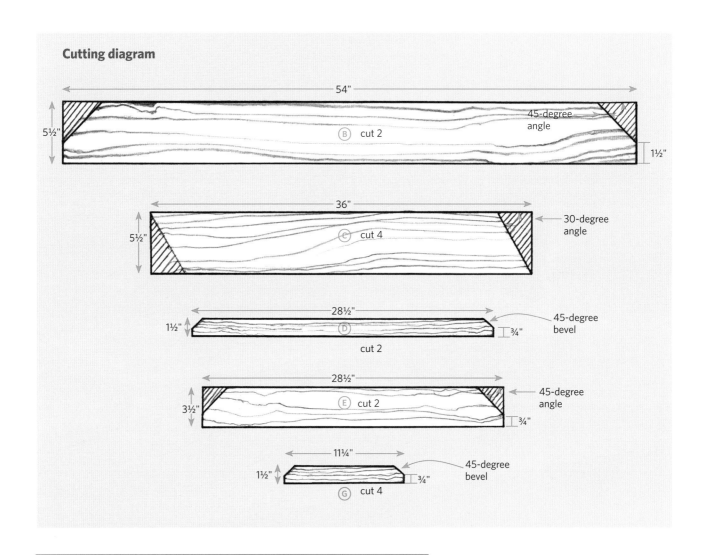

BUILDER'S TIP

When constructing a picnic table, cedar has long been a popular choice, and with good reason. Its dense texture makes it a stable wood that tends not to warp, and its natural oils not only inhibit rot and insect damage but also lend the wood a rich luster and pleasant aroma.

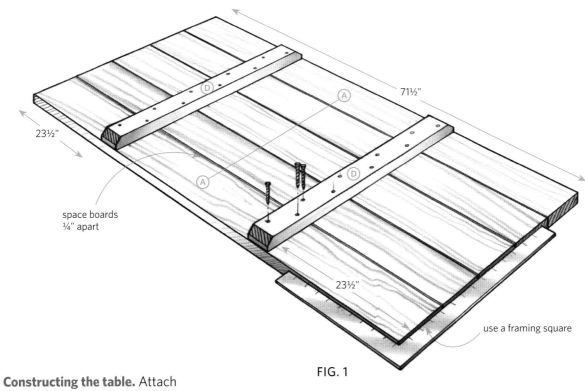

71½"

23½"

space boards
¼" apart

23½"

use a framing square

FIG. 1

Constructing the table. Attach
the two inner battens Ⓓ to the
underside of the tabletop boards
Ⓐ, as shown in fig. 1. Flip the
tabletop over, and attach the
outer battens, as shown in fig. 2.

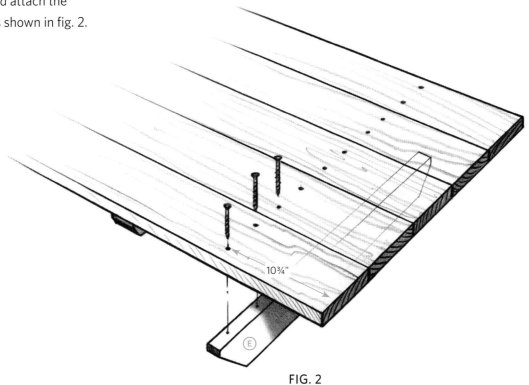

10¾"

FIG. 2

Turn the tabletop upside down once again, and attach the legs Ⓒ to the outer battens Ⓔ. Center and attach the seat supports Ⓑ to the legs. (See fig. 3.) Reinforce the joints in the leg structures with carriage bolts. The center of each joint needs to have a countersunk hole ($7/8$"×$3/8$" deep) for the nut on the inside and be predrilled ($3/8$") for the bolt. To finish up the bottom, make sure the legs are positioned at a 90° angle to the top, and secure them with the angle braces Ⓕ, as shown in fig. 4.

Set up the seats the same way the tabletop went together, attaching the seat battens Ⓖ 23½" from the ends and spacing the seat boards Ⓐ ¼" apart. Screw the seats to the seat supports Ⓑ (there should be a 10" overhang on both ends). Round and smooth all rough and cut edges with the file and sandpaper.

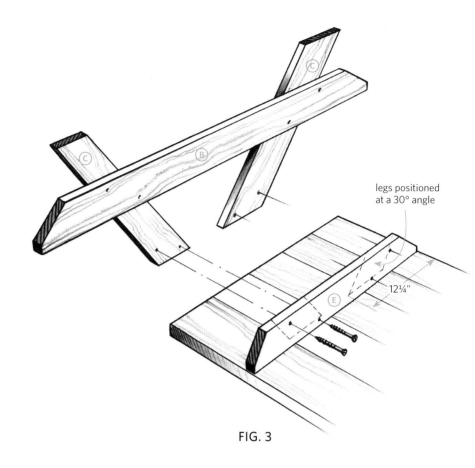

legs positioned at a 30° angle

12¼"

FIG. 3

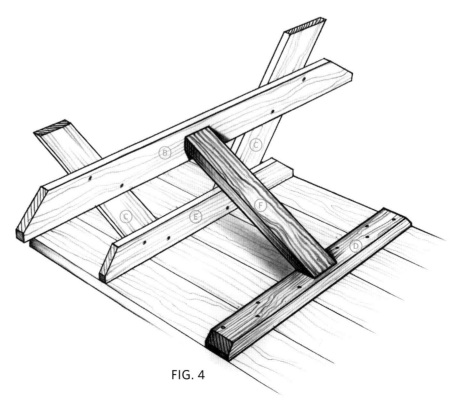

FIG. 4

Adirondack-Style Lawn Chair

If you've ever had the plastic pop under you as you sat in one of those ribbons-and-tubes chairs, you'll appreciate the sturdy comfort of this one. The spacious seat is contoured to support your back. And its roomy arms are handy for setting down a drink or the book you were reading before you began to nod off.

▲ ADIRONDACK-STYLE LAWN CHAIR. Its deep seat and reclined back make this solid lawn chair prime real estate on a summer's day.

MATERIALS

Lumber

⁵⁄₄"×6" cedar decking (five 10' lengths)

Supplies

2" stainless steel #8 pan-head Phillips screws (box of 100)

Eight 1½" stainless steel #8 pan-head Phillips screws

Tools

Tape measure

Pencil

Carpenter's square

Jigsaw

Power drill

⁵⁄₃₂" twist drill bit

Driver bit to match screws

Extension-bit holder (for attaching seat slabs)

Compass

Wood file

80-grit sandpaper

Helpful Bonus Tools

Power miter saw

Router with ¼" round-over bit

Table saw

Impact driver

Orbital sander

Cutting the lumber. From the ⁵⁄₄"×6", cut two each of slats Ⓐ, Ⓑ, Ⓒ, and Ⓓ, as shown in the cutting diagram. Cut two 34⅛" lengths for the rear legs Ⓔ and two 27¾" lengths for the arms Ⓕ, cutting to shape as shown in the cutting diagram. Continuing to follow the cutting diagram for board widths and shapes, cut one 24" length for the front stretcher Ⓖ, one 24" length for the curved back seat slat Ⓗ, eight 24" lengths for the seat slats Ⓘ, one 28" length for the center rib Ⓙ, one 24" length for the bottom rib Ⓚ, one 22" length for the top rib Ⓛ, two 10½" lengths for the arm brackets Ⓜ, and two 23¾" lengths for the front legs Ⓝ.

Cutting diagram

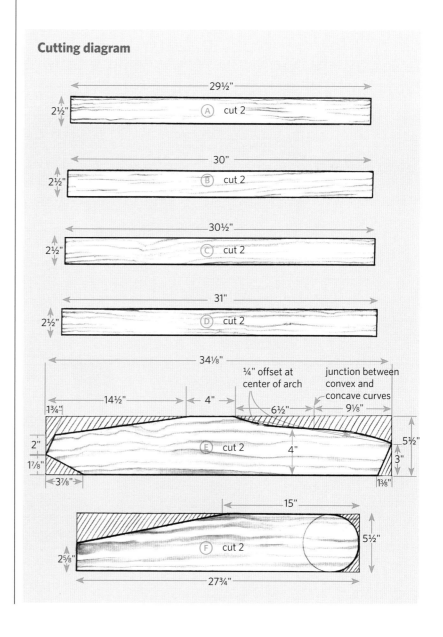

Cutting diagram

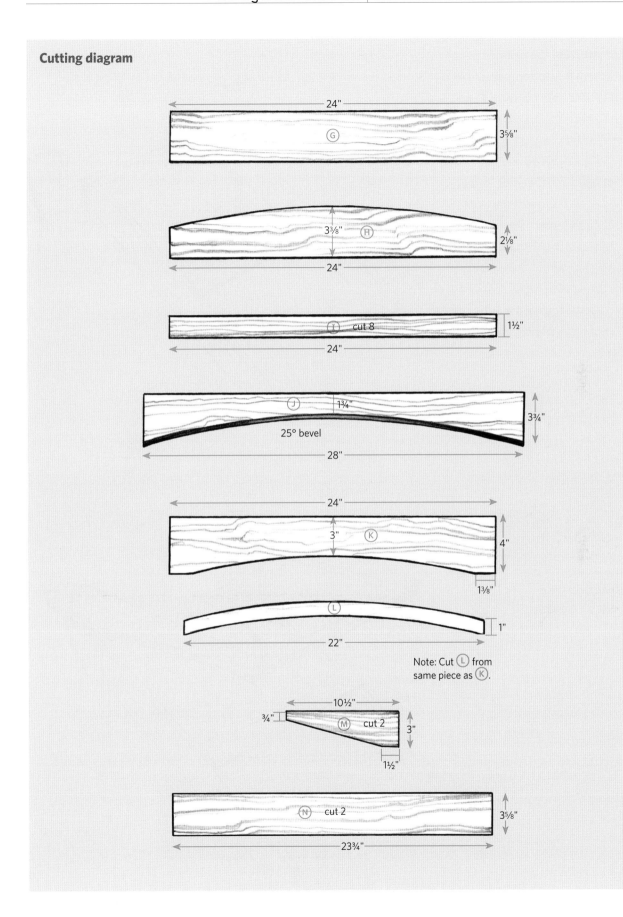

24"

G

3⅝"

3⅜"

H

2⅛"

24"

I   cut 8

1½"

24"

J   1¾"

25° bevel

3¾"

28"

24"

3"   K

4"

1⅜"

L

1"

22"

Note: Cut L from
same piece as K.

10½"

¾"   M   cut 2

3"

1½"

N   cut 2

3⅝"

23¾"

Constructing the chair. Start by attaching the bottom rib Ⓚ to the flat spot on the rear legs Ⓔ, and then attach the front stretcher Ⓖ. Next, attach the arm brackets Ⓜ to the front legs Ⓝ and fasten the front legs to the rear leg frame, making sure to avoid the front stretcher screws. (See fig. 1.)

Make up the U-shaped frame of the chair arms Ⓕ and center rib Ⓙ, and attach it by screwing through the tops of the arms into the front legs Ⓝ and brackets Ⓜ (fig. 2).

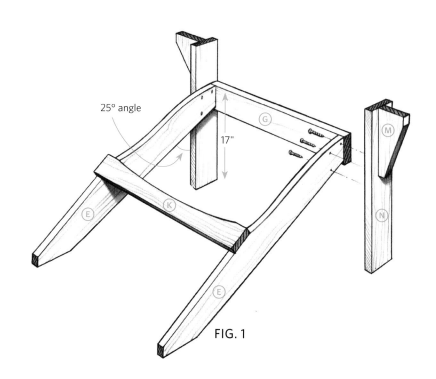

25° angle

17"

FIG. 1

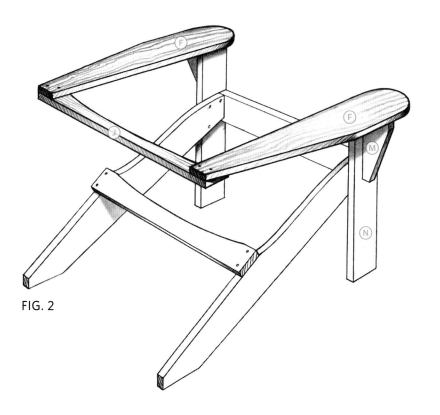

FIG. 2

Attach the back slats Ⓐ, Ⓑ, Ⓒ & Ⓓ (with the longer ones in the middle) to the center rib Ⓙ, flushing up the bottom edges and spacing the ribs ⅜" apart.

Then fasten the top rib Ⓛ from the back, positioning it 4½" down from the top of the center slats Ⓐ. (See fig. 3.)

Attach the seat slats to the rear legs Ⓔ, starting with the front one Ⓘ and the curved back one Ⓗ. Then center one of the remaining slats Ⓘ between them and infill the rest, spacing them ⅜" apart.

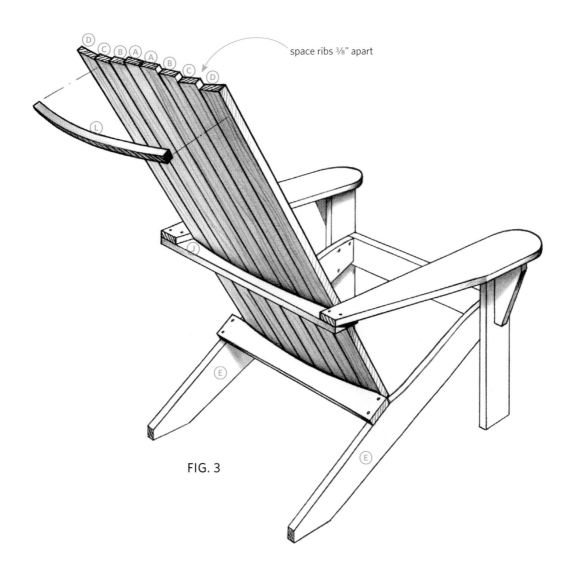

space ribs ⅜" apart

FIG. 3

Westport Chair

MATERIALS

Lumber

1"×10" cedar (10' length and 8' length)

1"×8" cedar (10' length and 8' length)

1"×4" cedar (10' length)

Supplies

1¼" stainless steel #8 pan-head screws

1¾" to 2" stainless steel #8 pan-head screws

Wood glue

Tools

Tape measure

Pencil

Large carpenter's square

24" level

Power drill

⅛" twist drill bit for pilot holes

Driver bit to match screws

Circular saw or ripsaw

½" chisel

T-bevel

Hammer

Jigsaw

Handsaw

Compass

This comfortable seat takes less time to build than the Adirondack chair, and it's not as heavy, so you'll find it easier to move about. The original design was the brainchild of Thomas Lee, who, in the early 1900s, created the chair to suit the terrain at his family's summer cottage in the village of Westport on the shores of Lake Champlain in New York State.

BUILDER'S TIP

If you'd like a rounded edge on the front seat slat — which can make your chair more comfortable where it presses against the back of your legs — bevel the top edge with a wood plane, then sand it smooth.

▲ WESTPORT CHAIR. The Westport chair was the precursor to the classic
Adirondack chair, built from fewer pieces and wider boards.

Cutting the lumber. From the 1"×10", cut one 39¼" length for a seat back slat Ⓐ, two 33½" lengths for stringers Ⓑ, two 32½" lengths for arms Ⓒ, and a 22" length for the middle seat slat Ⓓ.

From the 1"×8", cut a 39¼" length for a second seat back slat Ⓔ and two 12" lengths for the arm supports Ⓕ. From the remaining portion of 1"×8", you'll need a 22" length ripped to a 5½" width, with the back edge beveled 12°, for the back seat slat Ⓖ and a 16" length 1⅝" wide for the seat back batten Ⓗ.

From the 1"×4", cut a 29¾" length for an arm connector Ⓘ, two 24" lengths for legs Ⓙ, a 19½" length for a front leg brace Ⓚ, and an 18" length for the front seat slat Ⓛ.

Next, cut the stringers Ⓑ, the arms Ⓒ, the arm supports Ⓕ, and the notches in the front legs Ⓙ, as specified in the cutting diagram. Bevel the top edge of the arm connector Ⓘ 28° and the ends 45°.

Cutting diagram

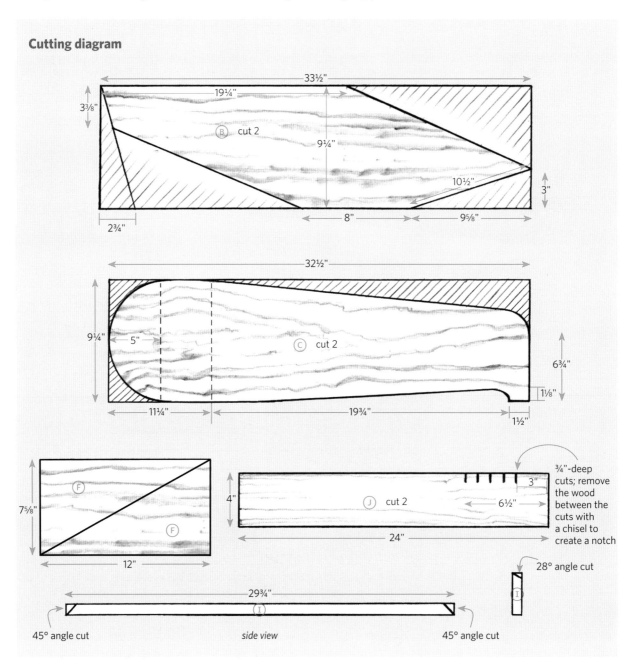

Constructing the chair. Attach the stringers Ⓑ to the front legs Ⓙ, squaring them up, as shown in fig. 1. Connect the legs by attaching the front seat slat Ⓛ and then fitting the leg brace Ⓚ into the notches and fastening the ends in place. Screw the remaining two seat slats Ⓓ & Ⓖ in place, first cutting ¾" angled notches in the 1"×10" board Ⓓ so it will fit snugly up against the legs. (See fig. 2.)

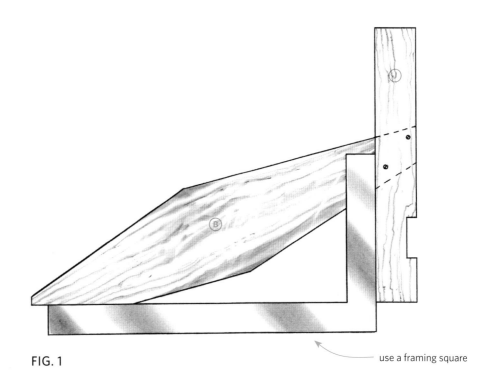

use a framing square

FIG. 1

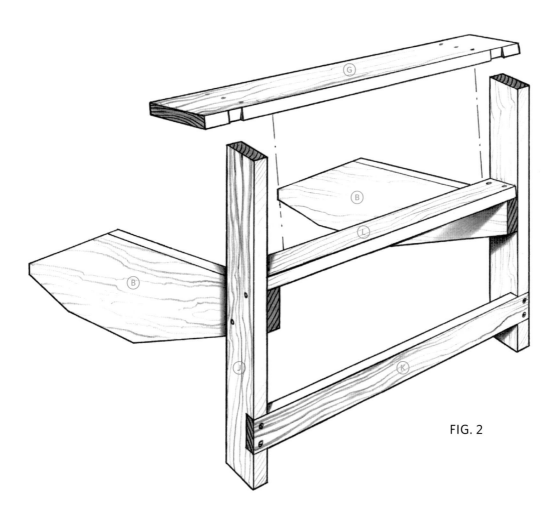

FIG. 2

Attach the seat back slats Ⓐ & Ⓔ to the back of the seat at a 12° angle, and fasten the triangular arm supports Ⓕ to the front legs Ⓙ. (See fig. 3.)

Attach the arm connector Ⓘ, determining the placement by placing the level on the arm supports Ⓕ and marking a level line on the seat back slats. (See fig. 4.) Attach the arms Ⓒ to the supports Ⓕ and the ends of the connector Ⓘ. Attach the seat back batten Ⓗ 3" down from the top of the slats.

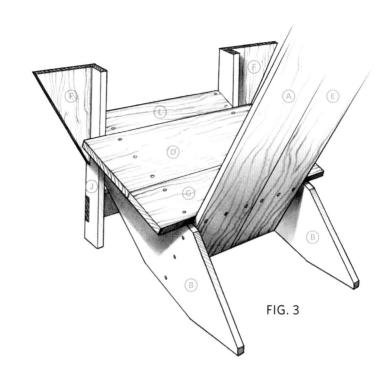

FIG. 3

position of seat back batten Ⓗ

3"

12° bevel

use level to determine placement of arm connector

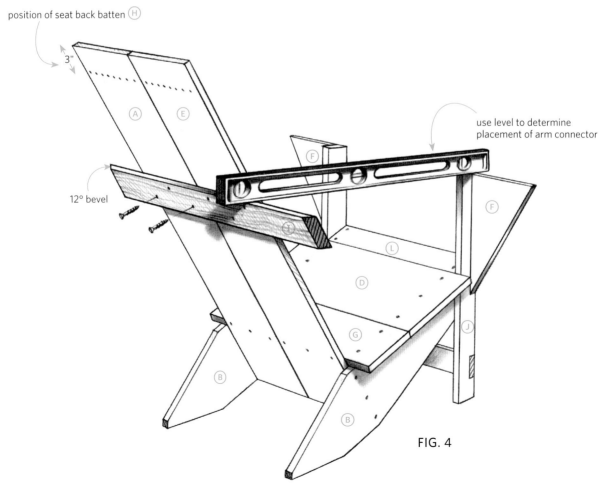

FIG. 4

Garden Swing

It seems sometimes that just the sight of a garden swing hanging from a tree limb overlooking a backyard or a garden can bring on a feeling of relaxation. With its contoured seat and back, this one really delivers. And it provides ample room for two.

▲ GARDEN SWING. A comfortable, roomy slatted seat makes this bench-style swing the ideal locale for swaying into a daydream.

MATERIALS

Lumber

5/4"×6" cedar (eight 10'
lengths)

Supplies

Four 3/8"×3" carriage bolts

Ten 3/8" nuts

Fourteen 3/8"×1" washers

#2/0×20' zinc-plated double-
loop chain with twisted
links (8' length)

Four 1/4" quick-link threaded
chain links

2" #8 pan-head stainless
steel screws (box of 100)

2 1/4" stainless steel trim-
head screws (80 or so)

Tools

Tape measure

Pencil

Speed square

Framing square

Compass

Circular saw with rip fence

Jigsaw

Power drill

1/8" twist drill bit for pilot
holes

3/8" drill bit for the bolt
holes

Driver bits to match screws

Adjustable wrench

Bolt cutter

Wood file

80-grit sandpaper

Helpful Bonus Tools

1/4" blocks for spacing the
seat slats

Table saw

Router with 1/4" flush round-
over bit

Orbital sander

6' stepladder (for hanging
the swing)

Cutting the lumber. From the
5/4"×6", cut two 24 1/8" lengths for
the arms Ⓐ & Ⓑ. Use the cutting
diagram as a guide to trim the
arms and also to cut the remain-
der of the lumber according to
the following key:

- Ⓒ seat support (cut 4)
- Ⓓ back support (cut 3)
- Ⓔ arm support (cut 4)
- Ⓕ arm post (cut 2)
- Ⓖ ceiling batten
- Ⓗ seat crest
- Ⓘ front plate with 9° beveled
     top edge
- Ⓙ back plate (cut 2)
- Ⓚ seat slat (cut 17)
- Ⓛ seat slat between posts
     (cut 2)

Cutting diagram

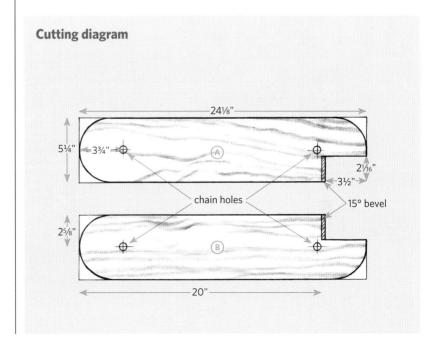

Cutting diagram

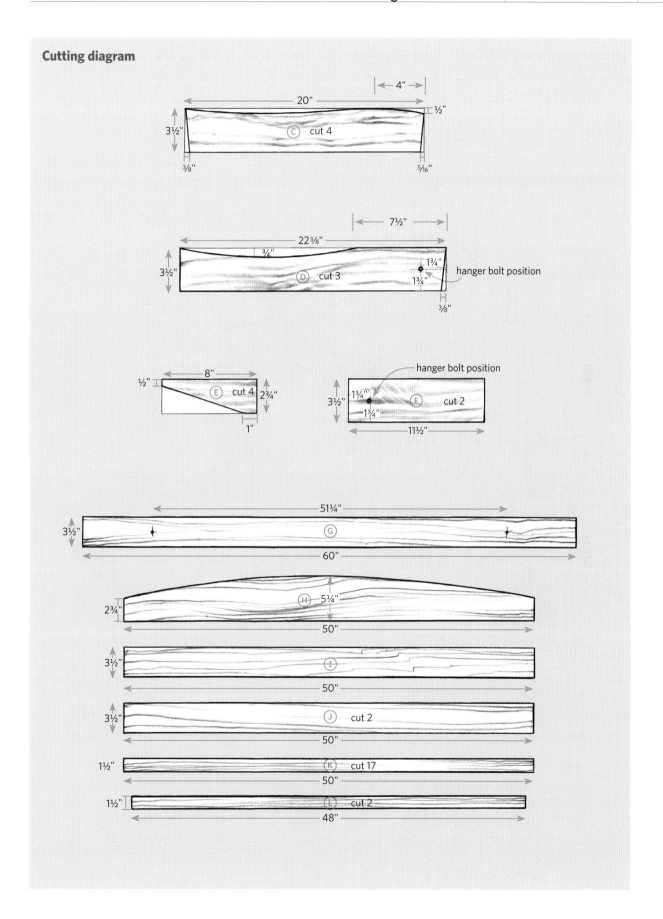

Constructing the swing. Make up the seat frame by attaching the front plate Ⓘ and one back plate Ⓙ to the four seat supports Ⓒ, as shown in fig. 1. Attach the second back plate Ⓙ to the tops of the three back supports Ⓓ. Then fasten the bottom of the back supports Ⓓ to the back ends of the seat supports Ⓒ, staying clear of the center on the corners. (This is where the hanging bolts will go.)

Attach the front arm supports Ⓔ to the arm posts Ⓕ, flushing them up at the top. Then fasten the bottom of the arm posts to the front corner of the outer seat supports Ⓒ, driving in screws from the front and the sides. (See fig. 2.)

To set up and attach each of the back arm supports Ⓔ, on each side use a level to square

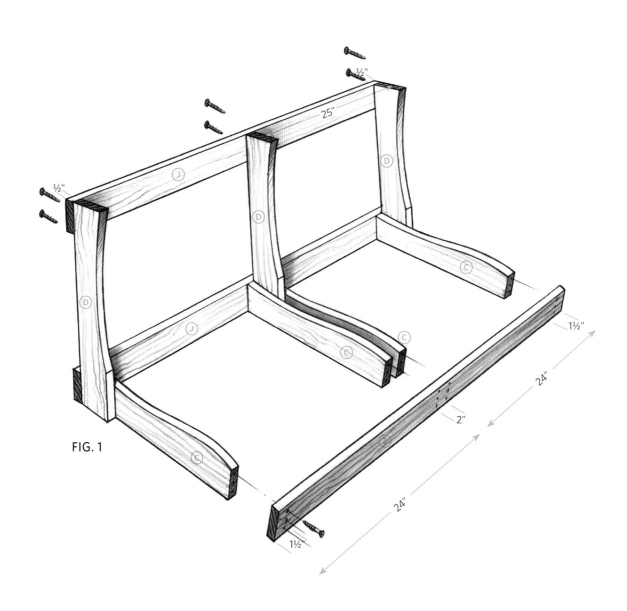

FIG. 1

across from the top end of the arm post Ⓕ and draw a line horizontally where you meet the back support Ⓓ, measure back ½", and mark and predrill pilot holes 2" and 5½" down along a line parallel to the front arm post Ⓕ. Position each back arm support in place, and screw through the back support Ⓓ into them.

Use the 2¼" trim-head screws to fasten down the seat slats Ⓚ & Ⓛ, spacing them ¼" apart. The first long seat slat Ⓚ registers against the front arms, right over the front plate Ⓘ, followed by the two short slats Ⓛ between the arm posts. Then finish up with long slats Ⓚ; they'll overhang the seat supports Ⓒ by 1" on each

end. When you start on the back of the seat, work from the bottom up, flushing up the ends, and finish off at the top with the seat crest Ⓗ.

Now fasten the arms Ⓐ & Ⓑ to the tops of the arm posts Ⓕ and arm supports Ⓔ and then to the back supports Ⓓ and adjacent slat ends Ⓚ.

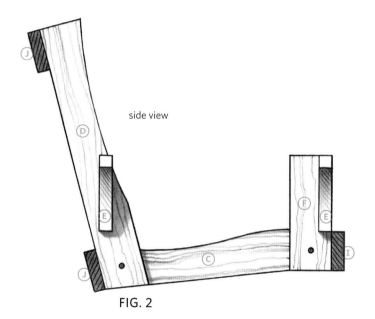

side view

FIG. 2

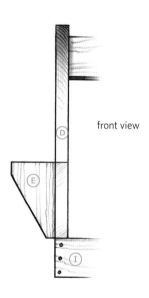

front view

BUILDER'S TIP

If you don't have bolt cutters, you can ask the hardware store clerk about having the chain cut to the lengths you need.

Set up the hanging bolts by drilling four ³⁄₈" holes 1¾" in and 1¾" up on the bottoms of the arm posts Ⓕ and back supports Ⓓ, as specified in the cutting diagram. Insert carriage bolts from the inside, so their ends extend out from the seat frame, and tighten them down with washers and nuts. Next, drill two holes to accommodate the chains in each arm Ⓐ & Ⓑ, as specified in the cutting diagram. (Round over the edge of the holes with a file and sandpaper.) On each side of the swing, attach the individual chain lengths to the carriage bolts by sandwiching the last link between a pair of washers, slipping the assembly onto the bolt, and then tightening it down with a nut. Use quick links to join the short and long chain lengths on each side of the swing.

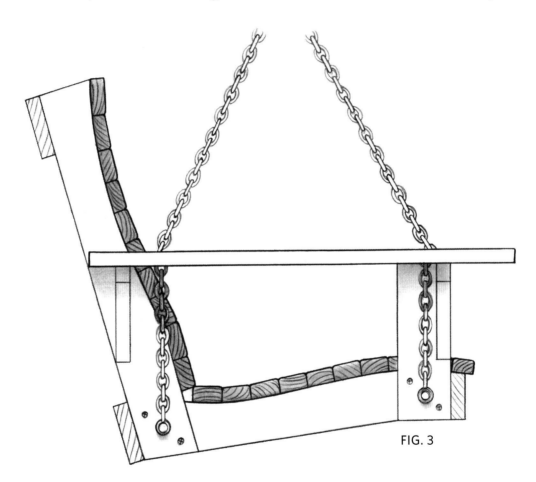

FIG. 3

Hanging Your Swing

Using a ceiling batten Ⓖ to hang your swing will give you greater flexibility when choosing a location. You can easily make one from a 5' length of 2"×4" by attaching a pair of sturdy eyebolts to it with nuts that are recessed into the top of the board. Keep in mind that the seat should be between 16" and 20" above the ground, which means that if you're mounting the swing to an 8' ceiling, you'll want a pair of 80" chain lengths for the back and a pair of 40" lengths for the front. You'll also need four quick links for attaching the chains to the eyebolts, as well as for creating the chain junctures on both sides of the swing. The front chains connect to the back chains about half-way up, depending on how you choose to angle the seat. Also, make sure you leave ample space behind the swing!

Pitched-Roof Birdhouse

MATERIALS

Lumber

1"×8" cedar (5' length)

2" wide stock (18" length) for the mounting board

Supplies

1⅝" #1 stainless steel trim-head screws (25 or so)

1¼" stainless steel pan-head screw (release for pivoting side)

Two 2½" stainless steel pan-head screws (for mounting)

Tools

Tape measure

Pencil

Carpenter's square

Wood saw

Power drill

1½" spade bit or other size appropriate for the bird species

⅛" twist drill bit

¼" twist drill bit

Driver bits to match screws

Wood glue

Besides being a cheery presence in your yard, birds can be a real asset when it comes to keeping insects from wreaking havoc in your garden — although the birds may also help themselves to some of your produce, such as strawberries, grapes, and cherries. If you want to attract birds, installing birdhouses is a good start, as is planting trees, shrubs, or vines that offer them food. When boring the entrance hole, keep in mind that if it's too big the birds could be vulnerable to attack or displacement by larger birds. See the table on page 129 for the proper dimensions for different species.

▲ PITCHED-ROOF BIRDHOUSE. This tidy birdhouse includes a pivoting
side panel to provide access to the interior for easy cleaning.

Cutting the lumber. From the 1"×8", use the cutting diagram to cut all pieces according to the key at right:

Ⓐ front and back (cut 2, but drill entrance hole in front only)

Ⓑ sides (cut 2)

Ⓒ floor

Ⓓ longer roof board

Ⓔ shorter roof board

Cutting diagram

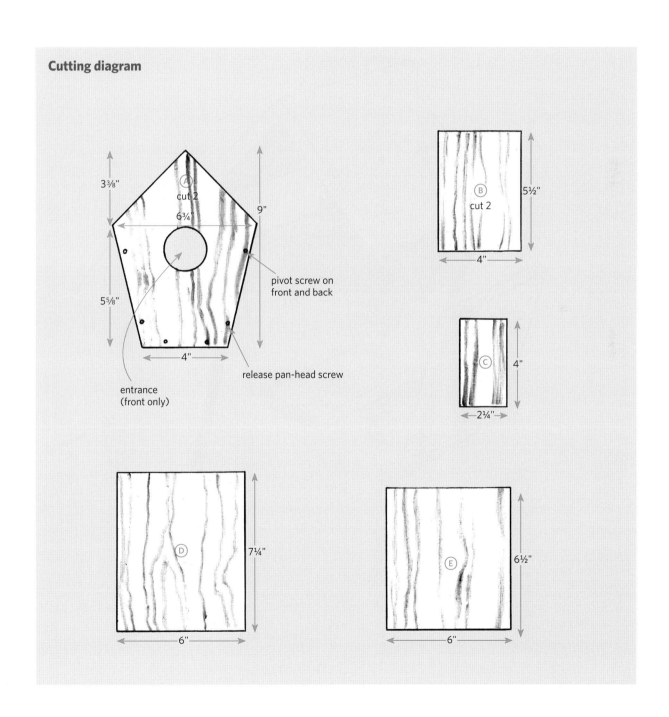

Constructing the birdhouse. Screw the front and back Ⓐ to the sides Ⓑ and floor Ⓒ. On the pivoting side, set the upper screws on the front and back Ⓐ directly opposite each other. Use a single 1¼" pan-head screw to fasten the bottom of the front to the side Ⓐ; do not fasten the bottom of the back to the side. This will allow the side panel to pivot open for cleaning when you release the pan-head screw.

Next, attach the top of the longer roof board Ⓓ to the edge of the shorter one Ⓔ. Then fasten the assembled roof to the top of the house.

Finally, fasten the mounting board Ⓕ to the back of the house. Mount the house in its location using 2½" screws.

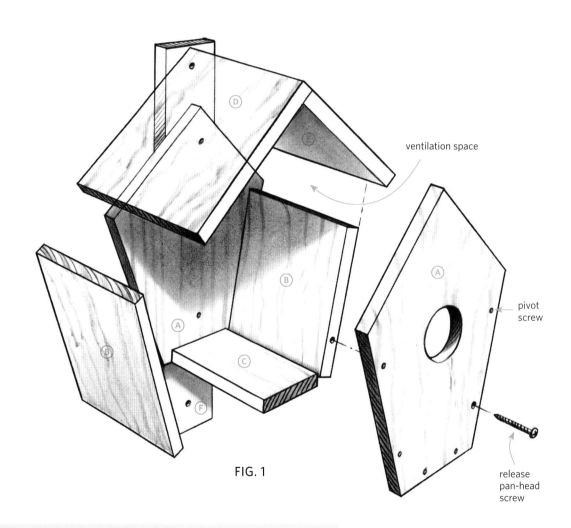

ventilation space

pivot screw

release pan-head screw

FIG. 1

Siting Birdhouses

When picking a location for your birdhouse, of course you'll want to make sure it is inaccessible to cats and other predators and that it does not face the prevailing wind. Nor should it tilt upward (lest the rain enter it). Also, keep in mind that birds have a strong territorial instinct, and several houses close together will only promote ill feelings among neighbors. (See also Providing Egress, page 132.)

A TABLE OF DIMENSIONS

Nesting Platforms (one or more sides open)

Bird	Minimum Floor Size	Box Depth	Preferred Ht. above Ground
Barn Swallow	6"×6"	6"	8'-12'
Phoebe	6"×6"	6"	8'-12'
Robin	6"×8"	8"	6'-15'
Song Sparrow	6"×6"	6"	1'-3'

Birdhouse

Bird	Floor Size	Box Depth	Ht. of Entrance above Floor	Entrance Diameter	Ht. above Ground
Bluebird	5"×5"	8"	6"	1½"	5'-10'
Chickadee	4"×4"	8"-10"	6"-8"	1⅛"	6'-15'
Crested Flycatcher	6"×6"	8"-10"	6"-8"	2"	8'-20'
Flicker	7"×7"	16"-18"	14"-16"	2½"	6'-20'
House Finch	6"×6"	6"	4"	2"	8'-12'
Nuthatch	4"×4"	8"-10"	6"-8"	1¼"	12'-20'
Owls					
Barn	10"×18"	15"-18"	4"	6"	12'-18'
Saw-whet	6"×6"	10"-12"	8"-10"	2½"	12'-20'
Screech	8"×8"	12"-15"	9"-12"	3"	10'-30'
Purple Martin	6"×6"	6"	1"	2½"	15'-20'
Sparrow Hawk	8"× 8"	12"-15"	9"-12"	3"	10'-30'
Starling	6"×6"	16"-18"	14"-16"	2"	10'-25'
Titmouse	4"×4"	8"-10"	6"-8"	1¼"	6'-15'
Violet-Green Swallow and Tree Swallow	5"×5"	6"	1"-5"	1½"	10'-15'
Wood Duck	10"×18"	10"-24"	12"-16"	4"	10'-20'
Woodpeckers					
Downy	4"×4"	8"-10"	6"-8"	1¼"	6'-20'
Golden Fronted and Redheaded	6"×6"	12"-15"	9"-12"	2"	12'-20'
Hairy	6"×6"	12"-15"	9"-12"	1½"	12'-20'
Wrens					
Bewick's Carolina	4"×4"	6"-8"	4"-6"	1¼"	6'-10'
House	4"×4"	6"-8"	4"-6"	1"-1¼"	6'-10'

Hinged-Roof Birdhouse

Here's a birdhouse that children can help build, so it's a good project if you have a budding carpenter in your flock. And the roof opens wide, providing plenty of room for small hands to access the inside for cleaning.

MATERIALS

Lumber
1"×6" cedar (4' length)
1"×8" cedar (8" length)

Supplies
Sixteen 1⅝" stainless steel trim-head screws
Pair of 2"×2½" hinges with mounting screws
Four 2½" #8 pan-head stainless steel screws

Tools
Tape measure
Pencil
Carpenter's square
Power drill
⅛" twist drill bit
¼" twist drill bit
Drill bit to match appropriate entrance hole
Driver bits to match screws
Phillips screwdriver
Wood glue

▲ HINGED-ROOF BIRDHOUSE. Install this inviting little house in the spring, then sit back and watch the birds move in.

Cutting diagram

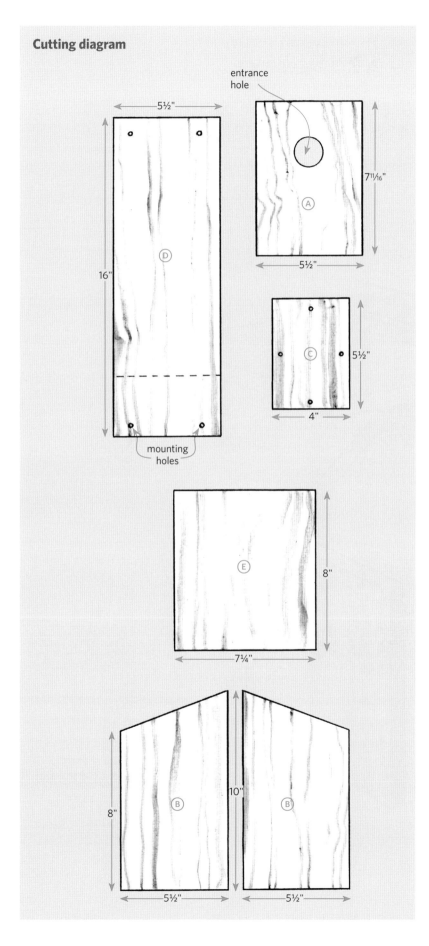

Cutting the lumber. From the 1"×6", cut one 7¹¹⁄₁₆" length for the front Ⓐ, two 10" lengths for the sides Ⓑ, one 4" length for the floor Ⓒ, and one 16" length for the back Ⓓ. Set the 1"×8" aside for the roof Ⓔ. Use the cutting diagram to shape the sides. Refer to the chart on page 129 to get the dimension and height above the floor for the entrance hole in the front Ⓐ, depending on the bird breed you hope to attract.

Constructing the birdhouse. Screw the front Ⓐ to the sides Ⓑ and floor Ⓒ. Then fasten the lower sides to the floor. Flip the assembly over, and attach the back Ⓓ so that 3" extends below the floor. Center the roof Ⓔ atop the house, and mount the hinges. Use pan-head screws to mount the house in the chosen location.

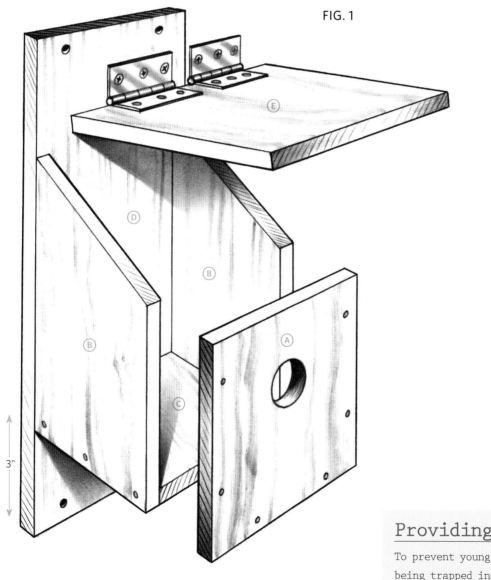

FIG. 1

Providing Egress

To prevent young birds from being trapped inside, score wood or add some rough material below the hole.

Nesting Platform

Robins, phoebes, and barn swallows will not use an enclosed birdhouse; they prefer a shelter with one or more open sides. Locate the platform in partial shade, perhaps hung from the main branch of a tree or under a shed or porch overhang 6' to 15' above the ground for robins, 8' to 12' for phoebes and barn swallows, and 1' to 3' for song sparrows. (See chart, page 129). To help the birds with their nest building, place some clay in a nearby puddle.

▼ NESTING PLATFORM. Robins, being particularly well adapted to suburban life, are the likeliest candidates to move into this backyard nesting platform.

MATERIALS

Lumber

1"×8" cedar (6' length)

Supplies

Two #10 pan-head exterior
   screws

Thirty 1⅛" stainless steel
   trim-head screws

Tools

Tape measure

Pencil

Carpenter's square

Circular saw or handsaw and
   miter box

Hand or power drill

¼" twist drill bit

⅛" twist drill bit

Phillips-head screwdriver
   or power drill fitted
   with screwdriver bit

Driver bits to match trim-
   head screws

Cutting the lumber. From the 1"×8", cut one 11½" length for the sides Ⓐ, one 8" length for the floor Ⓑ, one 14" length for the back Ⓒ, and one 9" length for the roof Ⓓ. Cut and trim the pieces as specified in the cutting diagram. From the remaining lumber, cut the side edging Ⓔ and front edging Ⓕ, as specified in the cutting diagram.

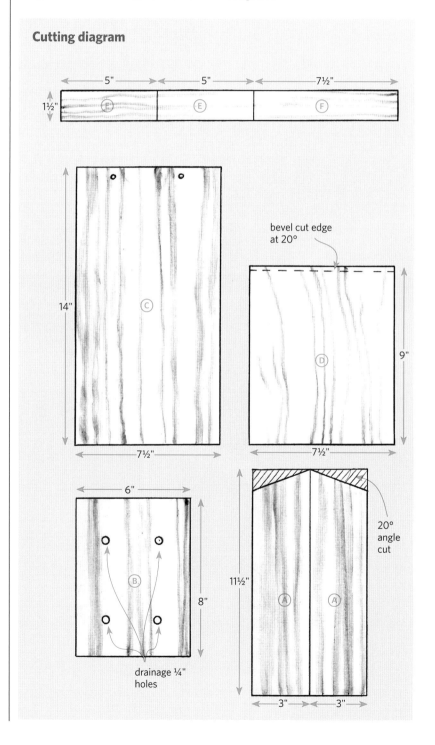

Cutting diagram

Constructing the platform. First screw the lower ends of the sides Ⓐ to the floor Ⓑ. Then attach the back Ⓒ, screwing through it into the sides and floor. Attach the roof Ⓓ, then fasten the side and front edging Ⓔ & Ⓕ in place.

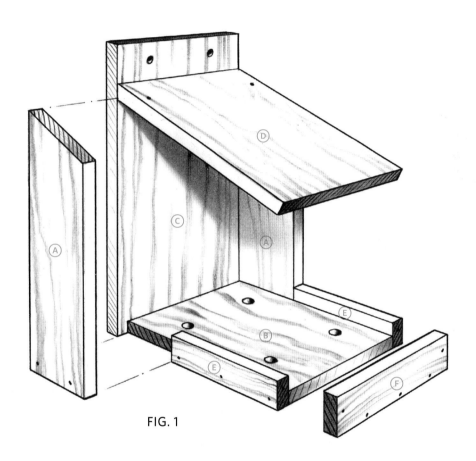

FIG. 1

BUILDER'S TIP

When building a platform for barn swallows and phoebes, the bottom should be a 6" square and the edging 3" high.

Platform Feeder

With an open tray that fastens directly to the top of the mounting post, feeding platforms don't get much simpler than this. One thing to keep in mind: You'll need to clean the platform regularly, removing bird droppings, seed hulls, and other debris.

▼ PLATFORM FEEDER. Installed above the ground, this style of feeder will attract not only ground feeders but also chickadees, cardinals, titmice, wrens, blue jays, blackbirds, and grosbeaks.

MATERIALS

Lumber

¾" CDX plywood (12"×18" rectangle and 1¾"×72" strip)

4"×4" cedar (7' length)

Supplies

6d galvanized nails (1-lb. box)

Four 2½" exterior pan-head screws

Tools

Tape measure

Pencil

Carpenter's square

Power drill

¼" and ⅛" twist drill bits

Screwdriver

Hammer

Cutting the lumber. From the plywood strip, cut two 19½" lengths for the front and back edging Ⓐ and two 12" lengths for the side edging Ⓑ.

Constructing the feeder. Drill four ¼" drainage holes in the corners of the 12"×18" feeder bottom Ⓒ. Nail the edging strips Ⓐ & Ⓑ in place. Screw down through the feeder bottom into the top of the 4"×4" cedar mounting post Ⓓ. Bury the bottom of the post 18" in the ground at your chosen location.

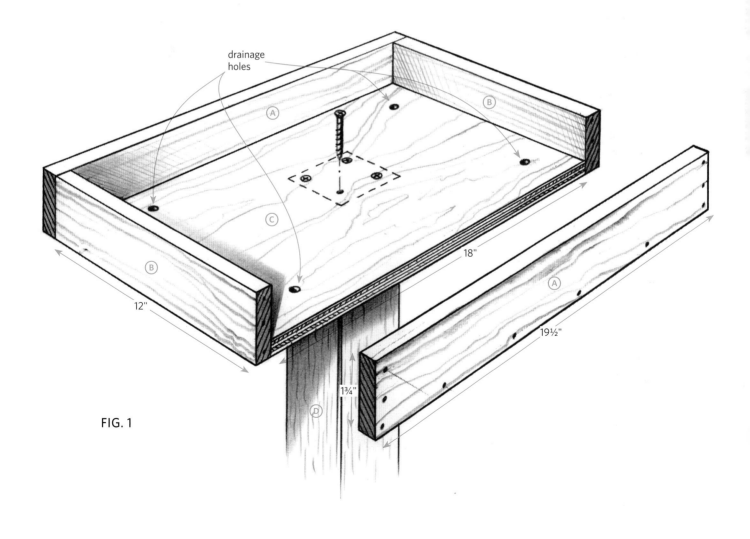

drainage holes

18"

12"

19½"

1¾"

FIG. 1

Single-Sided Hopper Feeder

▲ SINGLE-SIDED HOPPER FEEDER. These types of feeders are favorites of chickadees, titmice, nuthatches, and finches. They can be mounted on poles or trees or suspended from a wire to purposely create an unsteady perch that certain birds commonly considered pesky (such as house sparrows and blue jays) don't like.

Besides protecting the food from wind and rain, a hopper feeder such as this one can hold plenty of seed, so it doesn't need to be refilled often, and it's easy to clean. A hopper also lets you regulate the flow of seed by adjusting the size of the opening; however, if the opening is larger than ½", birds may push their heads through and get stuck.

MATERIALS

Lumber

1"×8" cedar (4' length)

Supplies

Two ¾" staples

Thirteen 1½" screws or 4d nails

⅛" acrylic (6"×3¾" piece)

2"×2" brass hinge with screws

Tools

Tape measure

Pencil

Carpenter's square

Circular saw

Power drill

¼" twist drill bit

Driver bit to match screws

Staple gun

Screwdriver

Cutting the lumber. Refer to the cutting diagram to cut all pieces according to the following key:

- Ⓐ back
- Ⓑ floor
- Ⓒ sides
- Ⓓ front closure strip
- Ⓔ side closure strips
- Ⓕ roof

Cut grooves in the sides Ⓒ as shown.

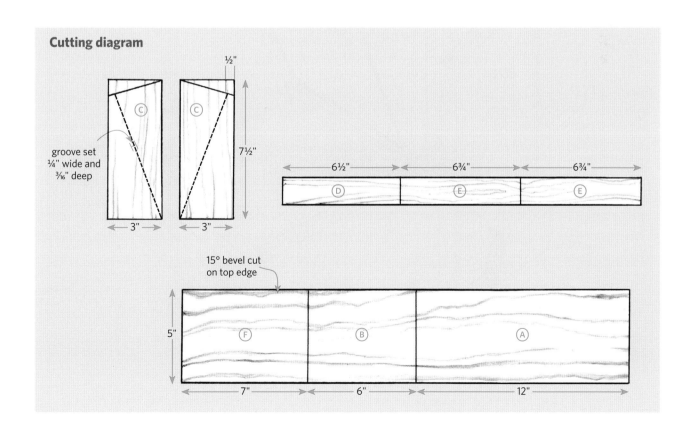

Cutting diagram

Constructing the feeder. Attach the feeder back Ⓐ to the floor Ⓑ. Screw the sides Ⓒ to the back and floor. Partially insert a staple across the groove on each side Ⓒ, ¾" up from the bottom (this will keep a small gap between the acrylic and the floor for seed to flow through). Note: It is important that the opening between the acrylic and the back of the box be no more than ½" to prevent birds from slipping through and getting caught inside. Adjust staples if necessary.

Attach the closure strips Ⓓ & Ⓔ to the floor. Center the roof Ⓕ atop the sides, and mount the hinge. With the roof open, slip the acrylic down into the side slots until the bottom comes to rest on the staples.

Mounting the single-sided hopper. Fill the hopper. Fasten the feeder in place by screwing through the mounting board.

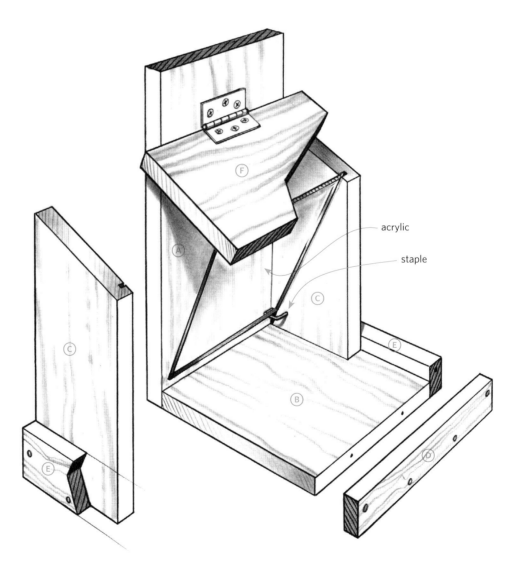

acrylic

staple

FIG. 1

Two-Sided Hopper Feeder

Compared with the one-sided hopper, the carpentry involved in building the two-sided hopper is a bit more complicated. However, it allows the mob to feed from both sides — certainly an advantage from the birds' point of view.

MATERIALS

Lumber
1"×12" (6' length)

Supplies
⅛" acrylic (two 6" squares)
Eight 4d nails
Twenty 1½" screws or 6d nails
Wood glue
15-gauge galvanized wire (3' length)
Continuous hinge (11" length cut into two 5½" lengths) with screws to go with it

Tools
Tape measure
Pencil
Carpenter's square
Circular saw
Hammer
Screwdriver
Hacksaw
Power drill
⅜" twist drill bit
Driver bit to match screws
Pliers

▲ TWO-SIDED HOPPER FEEDER. This feeder provides access from two directions — a feature that will have birds flocking to it in no time.

Cutting the lumber. Refer to the cutting diagram to cut all pieces according to the following key:

- Ⓐ stops (cut 2)
- Ⓑ sides (cut 2)
- Ⓒ spacer bar
- Ⓓ floor
- Ⓔ front and back closure strips (cut 2)
- Ⓕ side closure strips (cut 2)
- Ⓖ roof (cut 2)

Cut grooves in the sides Ⓑ as shown.

Cutting diagram

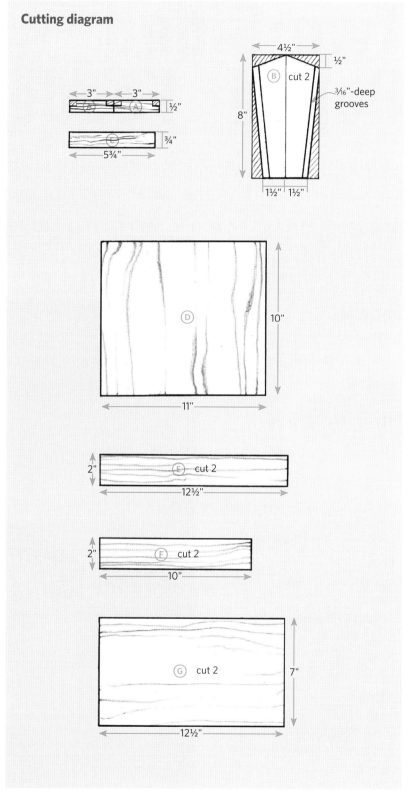

Constructing the feeder. Attach the stops Ⓐ to the bottom of the grooved sides Ⓑ, then connect the sides with the spacer bar Ⓒ. Center the assembly on the floor Ⓓ, and fasten it both from the top and the underside of the floor. Attach the closure strips Ⓔ & Ⓕ to the edges of the floor, and slip the acrylic squares down into the side slots.

Mount the hinge to the edges of the roof pieces Ⓖ to join them together. Place the hinged roof atop the sides, and nail one side of it in place.

For a hanger, drill down through the ridge of the roof between the hinges and through the spacer bar Ⓒ. Insert one end of the wire, and bend it into a hook below the spacer bar to keep it in place. Bend the top of the wire into a hook for hanging. (See fig. 2.)

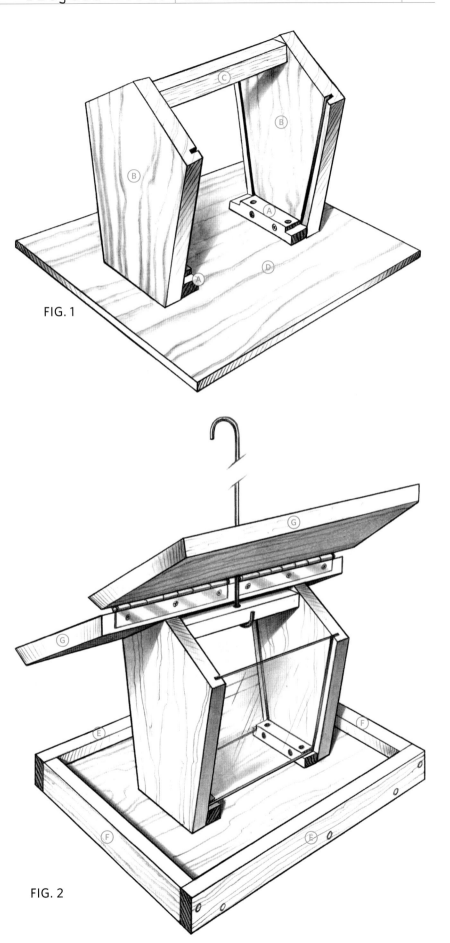

FIG. 1

FIG. 2

Weather Vane Feeder

MATERIALS

Lumber
1"×12" (6' length)

⅜" dowel (13¼" length)

Supplies
⅛" acrylic (6"×10½" piece)

Eighteen 1½" exterior wood screws

Lazy Susan turntable (9" diameter) with pre-drilled holes

Twelve ¾" #10 pan-head screws (for installing the lazy Susan)

Continuous hinge (cut to 12½" length) and screws to go with it

1" threaded galvanized pipe (8' to 10' length)

Galvanized pipe flange

Tools
Tape measure

Pencil

Carpenter's square

Circular saw

Screwdriver

Hacksaw

Power drill

¾" twist drill bit

Driver bits to match screws

Jigsaw

Sandpaper (optional)

Mounted to a turntable, the weather vane feeder rotates in the breeze and protects the seeds, although it may make your bird-watching dependent on which way the wind blows.

Locating and Maintaining Pole Feeders

As tempting as it is to locate a bird feeder close to a window, remember that birds don't recognize glass the way we do and will often fly right into it. Therefore, it is good practice to set a feeder at least several feet away from windows. To ensure the seed is reserved for birds only, install a squirrel baffle on the pole under the feeder, 3 or more feet above the ground. This is a better option than greasing or oiling the pole, since birds can't remove these substances from their feathers. Keep in mind that, like birdhouses, feeders should be cleaned regularly. This means removing moldy seeds and hulls as well as bird droppings.

▲ WEATHER VANE FEEDER. Designed to swivel away from the worst elements of weather, this feeder will minimize waste.

Cutting the lumber. Refer to the cutting diagram to cut all pieces according to the following key:

- Ⓐ stops (cut 2)
- Ⓑ sides (cut 2)
- Ⓒ back
- Ⓓ floor
- Ⓔ front roof
- Ⓕ back roof
- Ⓖ vanes (cut 2)
- Ⓗ mounting board

Cut grooves ³⁄₁₆" deep in each side Ⓑ, as shown in fig. 1.

Cutting diagram

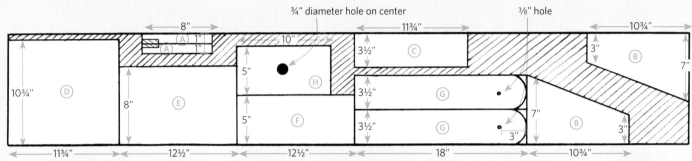

Constructing the feeder. Attach the stops Ⓐ, sides Ⓑ, and back Ⓒ to the feeder floor Ⓓ. Insert the acrylic into the grooves (see fig. 2). It is important that the opening between the acrylic and the back of the box be no more than ½" to prevent birds from slipping through and getting caught inside. Trim the stops if necessary.

Use the continuous hinge to join the two roof sections Ⓔ & Ⓕ. Screw the roof in place atop the sides (it should overhang the front by ½" and both sides by ³⁄₈"), being careful to avoid the acrylic window. (See fig. 3.)

Attach the vanes Ⓖ to the sides of the feeder, and tap in the dowel to connect them, as shown in fig. 3.

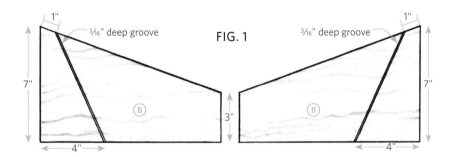

FIG. 1

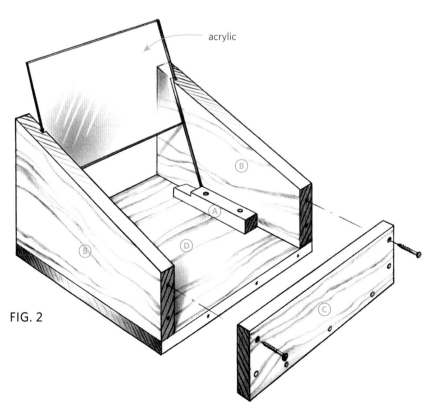

FIG. 2

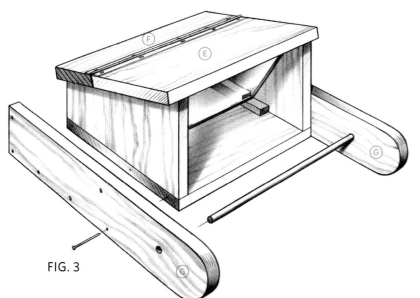

FIG. 3

Mounting the weather vane feeder to the lazy Susan. To install the feeder on the lazy Susan, you must first find the feeder's center of balance. You can do this by balancing it on a bottle cap set on a flat surface. Mark the point on the underside of the feeder. Next, center and attach the top plate of the turntable atop the mounting board (H).

With the feeder upside down, set the top plate assembly on top of it. To be sure the pieces are properly aligned, line up the mark you made on the feeder with the hole in the mounting board. Attach assembly to bottom of feeder. Screw the pipe flange to the board (around the center hole). (See fig. 4; for more detail on installing the lazy Susan, refer to manufacturer's directions.)

Set the bottom of the pipe into the ground, then screw the flange (and feeder) onto the pipe.

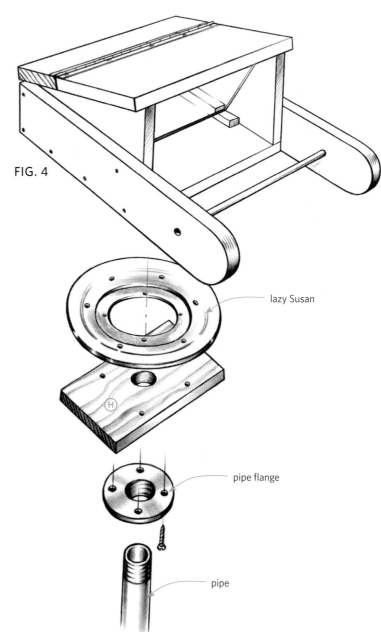

FIG. 4

lazy Susan

pipe flange

pipe

Flower Press

It's certainly simple enough to press a blossom or two by tucking them between the pages of a thick book. But a press such as this one is very easy and inexpensive to make, and because it applies even pressure, you will get better results. Once the flowers are dried, remove them from the press and store them for use in your projects.

▼ FLOWER PRESS. This hand-built model is a bit larger and heavier than most of those that are commercially available, so you can press a fair number of blossoms at a time.

MATERIALS

Lumber

¾" plywood (two 12" squares)

1"×2" pine or cedar (two 12" lengths)

Supplies

Four 6"×¼" carriage bolts (with rounded heads for flush mounting)

Four 1" flat washers with ¼" hole

Four ¼" wing nuts (with large wings for easy tightening)

1½" wood screws

Tools

Tape measure

Pencil

Carpenter's square

Power drill

⅜" twist drill bit

Driver bit to match screws

Wood saw

Hammer

Constructing the flower press. Mark and drill the locations for the four carriage bolts on the two plywood squares Ⓐ and two wood strips Ⓑ. (See fig. 1.) Insert the bolts through the holes in the wood strips, and use a hammer to tap the heads until they are flush with the boards. Place the strips parallel to each other with the thread ends of the bolts up, as shown in fig. 2, and fit the plywood squares in place, threading the bolts through the corner holes. Slip a washer onto each bolt, and tighten the assembly with the wing nuts.

Using the press. Cut two or more pieces of corrugated cardboard 8" square. Place one piece of cardboard on the bottom plywood square and cover it with a piece of paper towel or other absorbent material. Lay out your botanical material on the paper towel, cover with another piece of paper towel, followed by a piece of cardboard. Add as many additional layers of cardboard and paper as you wish, then put the top plywood square in place and use the wing nuts to apply pressure to the layers. If you're interested in drying only one or two layers at a time, use shorter carriage bolts.

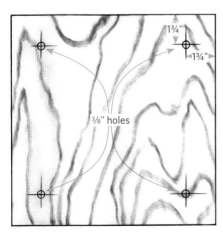

FIG. 1

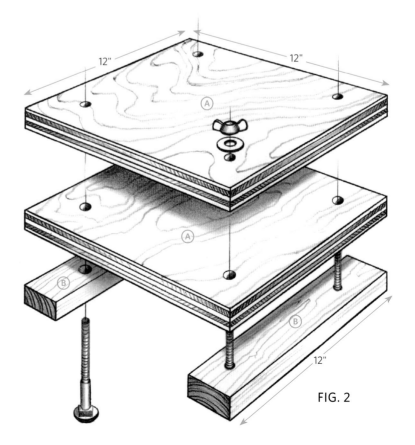

FIG. 2

Index

italic = illustration
bold = chart

Other Storey Titles You Will Enjoy

The Complete Compost Gardening Guide, by Barbara Pleasant & Deborah L. Martin.
Everything a gardener needs to know to produce the best compost, nourishment for abundant, flavorful vegetables.
320 pages. Paper. ISBN 978-1-58017-702-3.

Fences for Pasture & Garden, by Gail Damerow.
Sound, up-to-date advice and instruction to make building fences a task anyone can tackle with confidence.
160 pages. Paper. ISBN 978-0-88266-753-9.

How to Build Animal Housing, by Carol Ekarius.
An all-inclusive guide to building shelters that meet animals' individual needs: barns, windbreaks, and shade structures, plus watering systems, feeders, chutes, stanchions, and more.
272 pages. Paper. ISBN 978-1-58017-527-2.

Starter Vegetable Gardens, by Barbara Pleasant.
A great resource for beginning vegetable gardeners: 24 no-fail plans for small organic gardens.
192 pages. Paper. ISBN 978-1-60342-529-2.

The Vegetable Gardener's Bible, 2nd edition, by Edward C. Smith.
The 10th Anniversary Edition of the vegetable gardening classic, with expanded coverage and additional vegetables, fruits, and herbs.
352 pages. Paper. ISBN 978-1-60342-475-2. Hardcover. ISBN 978-1-60342-476-9.

The Veggie Gardener's Answer Book, by Barbara W. Ellis.
Insider's tips and tricks, practical advice, and organic wisdom for vegetable growers everywhere.
432 pages. Flexibind. ISBN 978-1-60342-024-2.

These and other books from Storey Publishing are available
wherever quality books are sold or by calling 1-800-441-5700.
Visit us at *www.storey.com*.